The
Gnostics

'This is the Universe. BIG, isn't it?'

(Michael Powell and Emeric
Pressburger, 1946)

The
Gnostics

Tobias Churton

WEIDENFELD AND NICOLSON
in association with Channel Four Television Company Limited
and Border Television plc

To the memory of Canon Aleric Rose
This Book is Dedicated with Love

Illustrations, except where indicated, and television series
Copyright © Border TV 1987
Text Copyright © Tobias Churton 1987

Published in Great Britain by
George Weidenfeld & Nicolson Limited
91 Clapham High Street
London SW4 7TA

ISBN 0 297 79106 0

Printed in Great Britain by
Butler & Tanner Ltd, Frome and London

The verse on page 73 is from *When We Were Very Young* by A. A. Milne.
Copyright 1924 by E. P. Dutton, renewed 1955 by A. A. Milne. Reprinted by
permission of the publisher, E. P. Dutton, a division of NAL Penguin Inc.

Contents

Introduction

Way back in March 1982 in the year of the ra-ra skirt and the Falklands war, I went for an interview with Diana Potter, Executive Producer at Thames TV. I was trying to be as fresh and enthusiastic as I could be after nine months on the dole. I'd got it into my head that there had never been any religious television – only programmes about religion. I had written a paper on the subject which recommended a new kind of television for this most neglected area, something on the lines of tele*vision*, a kind of programme which would enter into the very nature of the religious experience and not simply observe it. At the same time the paper suggested different forms of analysis of religious questions. Anyhow, in the course of the conversation I happened to mention Blake's famous 'Ancient of Days' painting – the one with the crouching bearded figure whose fingers reach downwards to the depths and divide it all up, erroneously regarded as Blake's picture of 'God' whereas it is only the Demiurge described by Plato as the creator, and by Blake as the builder of abstractions. I asserted 'Blake was a Gnostic' to which Diana Potter replied, 'Oh, are you interested in the Gnostics? John Ranelagh at Channel 4 is also interested in them. I'm having lunch with John on Monday and I'll tell him about you.' And so the long haul began.

On 6 April I entered the still unfinished Channel 4 building on Charlotte Street in London's West End and met John Ranelagh, then Commissioning Editor for Religious Programmes. John had had the idea of doing something based on Elaine Pagels' book *The Gnostic Gospels* which dealt with the discovery of a Gnostic library in Upper Egypt in 1945 and which promoted questions about the origins of the Christian Church and the validity of traditional expressions of Christian doctrine. I had had it in my mind that 'Gnosis' (Greek for 'knowledge' in the sense of interior certainty or insight) was a philosophy in its own right which somehow got tangled up in the growth of the early Church. Furthermore, it had occurred to me in the previous three and a half years that the Gnostics were entitled to a history of their own rather than as being seen as heretical or as esoteric Christians.

I had heard the music of the Gnostics in all sorts of unexpected places.

I had heard strains in romantic poetry, I had heard it in Rimbaud, I had heard it in the music of Debussy. I felt the presence of a 'golden string' which I followed through the occult philosophies of the Renaissance, and among the Cathars of the twelfth century – I had seen it in the visionary paintings and engravings of William Blake, in the music and sayings of John Lennon, Jim Morrison and Jimi Hendrix – so many scattered sounds and voices resonating through the centuries. Searching for Gnosis was like searching for myself. I knew this melody from somewhere far away. I had been born deaf and remained so for nearly three years and yet, somehow I think that I had heard it even then. I had heard it all my life but I did not know where to place it. Nobody knew anything about it at school and for years this incoherence felt threatening, but an experience of love would always chase the fears away. Then at college I heard the word Gnosticism and my ears pricked up. From them on I had a 'tree' on which to hang the scattered knowledge – but the form of the tree was rather misshapen until John Ranelagh gave me the opportunity to think about it all in the context of a television programme.

I left Channel 4 that sunny morning with one intent: to write the story of 'The Gnostics' for television. By the end of the spring I had a format entitled 'The Search for the Gnostics' which consisted of five programmes which would take the viewer from the second century AD to the Middle Ages, the Renaissance, the eighteenth century, on to the Age of Revolutions and finally to our own times. This was going to be somewhat bigger and more expensive a programme than one about the 'Gnostic Gospels' of Nag Hammadi. Indeed, this was the case and I was sad to find that money would not be available yet, maybe not until 1985. That seemed a long way off. Perhaps it was all for the best because I spent the next three years not only in deepening my understanding about the subject matter but also in gaining experience as a television researcher and writer.

In the early summer of 1985, the thread was joined again and I heard that the project could now be funded and would be produced by Border Television. In the November of that year I was brought in to research the project which began filming in Egypt at the end of the winter of 1986.

I would rather not say any more about the programmes for fear of giving the game away before people have a chance to see the results of a year-and-a-half's televisual labour.

This book is intended to accompany the series, of course, but I also hope that it will be read in its own right for as long as it is right to do so. The story of Gnosis will doubtless occupy scholars and students for many years to come and all sorts of things will be discovered which will change our perspective of the matter. So much that is exciting often takes far too long to reach the general public for whom this book is primarily intended. For once the meal is not cold, the study of Gnosis is still in a crude state and so I hope readers feel free to indulge in their own speculations on the subject and add to what we know about it all. So much remains to be done.

Naturally I would never have embarked upon the project of bringing the Gnostic experience to a hungry public if I was not convinced that an understanding of the subject could 'change the world'. All it takes to do so is to imagine the world differently. That will certainly change your world. The integrity of your vision of the world is worth living for. Television and films and things may seem important but they are not *minds*. That's what you've got that no work of art can reproduce. I hope this book is good food for the mind. As the dormouse said, 'Feed your head'.

Just one last word. I wrote the section called 'A Mystery Tour' in Part Two with the idea in mind that readers may wish to visit the places mentioned within and perhaps relive the events described, in the imagination – the true home of reality. This you knew when you were children. Know it again.

Tobias Churton
4 November 1986
Oxford

Acknowledgments

I should first like to express my indebtedness to Border Television and Channel 4 Television without whose courage this book would be only a shadow of what I hope it is. In particular, the Producer of the series, Steve Segaller, Border's Programme Controller Paul Corley, Border's Managing Director Jim Graham, the cameramen Tom Ritchie and Eric Scott Parker and all of the splendid crew and administrative staff. At Channel 4, John Ranelagh and Peter Flood whose encouragement in times of despair has been invaluable.

Secondly, I acknowledge indebtedness to all those people who gave time and energy in interviews, discussions and hospitality. They are Professor R. McLachlan Wilson of St Andrews, Professor Hans Jonas of New Rochelle, New York, Professor Elaine Pagels of Princeton, Professor Gilles Quispel of Bilthoven in Holland, Professor R. I. Moore of Sheffield University, Professor Alexander Murray of New College Oxford; Deputy Librarian of the Bodleian Library, Oxford, Julian Roberts; Anne Brenon, Director of the Centre Nationale d'études Cathares in Villegly, France; Patrick Clanet also of the Cathar Study Centre; Gérard Zuchetto and Patrice Briant – living troubadours of Languedoc; Basil Wilby, Dr Kathleen Raine whose feeling for Blake is unparalleled; Professor Sidney Alexander of Florence and Professor Michel Rocquebert of Montségur.

Thirdly, a special acknowledgment must go to the staff of the Bibliotheca Philosophica Hermetica in Amsterdam: the Curator, Dr Frans Janssen, Frank Van Lamoen – brilliant scholar of Hermetism, José Bauman, and especially to Joseph Ritman, founder of this unique and wonderful library and who has made it possible for me to travel to Amsterdam to study there in perfect surroundings. Mr Ritman, a Gnostic if ever there was, believes that in gnosis, all limitations can be overcome – and his generosity has certainly helped me to overcome many. I should like to add here that the achievement of the Hermetic Philosophy Library is itself unique and deeply encouraging.

Lastly, I would like to thank all those who have made my difficult journey through the experience of this subject more bearable. In Germany: Gerhard Fitzthum, philosopher and friend; Heinz Reinhoffer,

Bernhard Antony, Gila Ohrenburg, Peter Damm. In England, the late and much loved Canon Aleric Rose – the kind of man the Church of England cannot replace; my mother and father, Victor and Patricia Churton; Jan Harris, who compiled the index; Michael Curtis, Dave Scott, Belinda Parsons, Caroline Hewitt, Belona, Mike Shaw, Graham Whitlock, Cathy Palmer, Christian Wangler, Sarah Miller, Roger Stott, Dalia Johananoff, Roger Hooker, Caroline Sherwood, George Simey, Jackie Hill and the love and inspiration I have received from the artist, Louise Ford.

I should also like to acknowledge my ready appreciation of the actors who brought spirit to the dead letters of drama scripts: Ian Brooker, Brian Blessed, Paul Dixie, Raymond Ross, James Tillett and the 'Gnostic Jesus', Nigel Harrison.

All quotations from the Nag Hammadi Library are taken from *The Nag Hammadi Library* translated into English under the Editorship of James M. Robinson, published by E. J. Brill of Leiden (1977).

To all the above and all those visible and invisible unnamed, a heart-filled Thank you.

> I trod the rounded tiny debris
> of past and new construction,
> And wondered,'Who could build
>   'this basilica of eternity?'
> Turning back, as one, the few who shun
> Modernity.
>   (From *The Rock*. Carcassonne 1979)

Illustration Acknowledgments

The photographs in this book are reproduced by kind permission of the following: the Bibliotheca Philosophica Hermetica, Amsterdam 11 below, 12, 13, 14, 15, 16; the Bodleian Library, Oxford 11 above; Ian Brooker 8 left; Patrick Clanet 6, 7, 8 below, 9 above, 10 below; Jim Davies 8 right; Mike Dodd 1, 2, 3, 4; Kate O'Sullivan 5, 9 below. The maps on pages 10 and 77 are by Richard Natkiel Associates, and the illustration on page 11 appeared in *Rivista di Archeologia Christiana* XXI (1944/5), 164 221, p. 185.

PART ONE

Gross Bodies

Chapter One

Gross Bodies

Their natures fiery are, and from above,
And from gross bodies freed, divinely move.
(Vergil on the Celestial Virtues
quoted in 1651 translation of
Henry Cornelius Agrippa's
Three Books of Occult Philosophy, 1531)

The world was still at war with itself when in the year AD 367 an instruction came to the monastic community at Tabinnisi. The head of the community, Theodore, was instructed to read the 39th Festal Letter of the Bishop of Alexandria, Athanasius. Perhaps the instruction had come from Alexandria. Such a thing would be expected from a senior bishop who had already struck fear and hatred into the deviant hearts of the unorthodox, the heretics, on many occasions. Tabinnisi was some 500 miles down the Nile from Alexandria. It was remote from the full weight of authority and Big Trouble often starts in the remote places. It is unlikely that the instruction was for the ears of the community alone. Its pioneering founder, Pachomius, had within living memory set up a rule to unite disparate and solitary people within a community whose practice of strenuous labour involved a strict, almost military discipline. The Christian life was not to be for the elevation of the individual soul alone. The Church had found that the message of love for one's neighbour, promulgated by Christ himself, could blend with and yet further ennoble that civic responsibility and state-duty which was so dear and necessary to the Roman Imperium. Faraway places, even in upper Egypt were never too far away from the voice of authority.

The members of this rather new community were ascetics, that is, they held that the needs and sensations of the body interrupted the essential communion with God for which the human community existed. Pleasure, leisure, food, sex and property were, therefore, thoroughly suspect. One may even say that they were feared. That modern psychology which deals with liberation from repression can find words to express the condition of Pachomius's more famous contemporary, Antony (250–356). Leaving behind both family ties and attendant property, Antony ventured outside of society and into the desert of Upper Egypt: the Thebaid. There he became prey to demonic visitations of an intensely suggestive nature, particularly with regard to sexual arousal. The more he tried to beat off the attack, the more strongly did Satan's agents return with the fire of lust. Thus, the threatening power of the body was for him and his spiritual descendents confirmed. Each rebuff of the body's call was felt as a victory for Christ and as an advance on the solitary path to holiness. Men were at war with themselves in the desert because the world was at war with itself. Saint Paul had made this clear enough:

> For the earnest expectation of the creation waiteth for the revealing of the sons of God. For the creation was subjected to vanity, not of its own will, but by reason of him who subjected it, in hope. That the creation itself shall be delivered from the bondage of corruption into the liberty of the glory of the children of God. For we know that the whole creation groaneth and travaileth in pain together until now.
>
> (Epistle to the Romans VIII. 19–22.)

The Peace of God, experienced on the retreat of the demonic enemy, was proof positive of the power of Christ. The attainment of that peace was a matter of the greatest urgency. The community life, withdrawing from the world into a simplicity, could give support to those engaged in this war. Furthermore, this new society, the monastic community with its visible head, provided doctrinal regulation so as to prevent the monk from being misled by the exercise of his solitary mind. Antony, in his solitude was deemed an exceptional case and Athanasius, who wrote a biography of Antony, was most keen to stress that the saint, for so he was to be remembered, had not departed from orthodoxy. Indeed, orthodoxy had enabled Antony to resist those Temptations with which his name has been most associated. Any man alone in the desert risked madness – and it was held that madness was an attribute of heresy which would threaten not only the salvation of the individual but also the existence of the Church. Orthodoxy means *right opinion* and it was a function of the bishop to keep his flock on the straight and narrow.

Thus it was that the instruction to translate, copy and distribute the

39th Festal Letter of Athanasius came to Theodore, head of the monastery at Tabinnisi. Theodore's responsibilities were not of course confined to the monastery proper but extended as far as his name and authority were known to the Christians of the Thebaid. In his 'patch' were many ascetics who were not interested in community life. They might assert that had they been in need of community, they would better have stayed in Luxor or Alexandria or Ephesus or wherever they came from. The attraction of the area lay surely in its distance from what appeared to be the main currents of civilization. Distance from the world was their aim. These outsiders might be static solitaries or wanderers alone or in groups. Anyhow, they resisted regulation and therefore identification and were doubtless regarded by those of orthodox inclinations with a sense of disturbance or suspicion. We may presume then that they were occasionally visible in towns and villages, sometimes among the ordered monks, often disappearing. As the organization of the monastery progressed they would doubtless become more visible in both the eye and mind.

What then was in the letter? To whom was it really addressed?

But since we have made mention of heretics as dead, but of ourselves as possessing the Divine Scriptures for salvation; and since I fear lest, as Paul wrote to the Corinthians, some few of the simple should be beguiled from their simplicity and purity, by the subtlety of certain men, and should afterwards read other books – those called apocryphal – led astray by the similarity of their names with the true books; I beseech you to bear patiently, if I also write, by way of remembrance, of matters with which you are acquainted, influenced by the need and advantage of the Church. In proceeding to make mention of these things, I shall adopt, to commend my undertaking, the pattern of Luke the evangelist, saying, Forasmuch as some have taken in hand, to reduce into order for themselves the books termed apocryphal, and to mix them up with the divinely inspired Scripture, concerning which we have been fully persuaded, as they who from the beginning were eyewitnesses and ministers of the word, delivered to the fathers; it hath seemed good to me also, having been urged thereto by the brethren, and having learned from the beginning, to bring before you the books included in the Canon, and handed down, and accredited as Divine; to the end that any one who has fallen into error may correct those who have led him astray; and that he who continues steadfast in purity, may again rejoice, having those things brought to his remembrance.

Athanasius goes on to list the Canon of literature which is to be accepted as authoritative and divine. We know this list as our Bible. For the Bishop of Alexandria,

These are the fountains of salvation, that he who thirsteth may be satisfied with the words they contain. In these alone is proclaimed the doctrine of godliness. Let no man add to them, neither let him take aught from them. For on this point the Lord put to shame the Sadducees, saying 'Ye do err, not knowing the Scriptures.' And He reproved the Jews, saying, 'Search the Scriptures, for they testify of Me.'

Athanasius asserts that none of the canonical or official scriptures refers to the apocryphal or unofficial writings, 'But this is an intention of heretics, writing them to favour their own views, bestowing upon them their approbation, and assigning to them a date, and producing them as ancient writings, that thereby they might find occasion to lead astray the simple.'

There we have it. The heretics exploited the simple. This will become a familiar pattern of accusation. It is strange to read the accusation today when many would argue that it is the Church which has and does exploit 'the simple' with gratifying fantasies and simplistic sermonizing. I suppose that it is a tendency of all those who regard themselves as authorities to regard the 'others' as either simple or dangerously pernicious. Indeed, a Church which makes peace with its enemies has already lost authority. The simple need to be protected from the pernicious – is this not the noble purpose of authority? But did not Jesus enjoin his apostles to feed his sheep – and not to put them on a diet?

Athanasius is suggesting I think that there may be some decent, that is simple people who may hold the works of pernicious men but the guilt and shame lies with the passer-on of the corrupt substance, and not with the receiver. They have been beguiled by the clever ones. Subtlety was the art of the serpent when he beguiled Eve with the fruit of the Tree of Knowledge of good and evil. Thus was mankind banished from simple communion with God. Athanasius says quite clearly that he is 'influenced by the need and advantage of the Church'. It was the work of the Church as the body of Christ to undo the damage done in Eden. But Eden was never called Heaven and a man must forever be beholden to Christ's Church for his salvation. He was not going back to Eden but somewhere else. The Church held the Keys to the Kingdom and the heretics, Athanasius says, are already dead.

The Burial

When Athanasius refers to the heretics as 'already dead', he means that they are outside that eternal life which is offered to the baptized Christian within the Catholic Church. The holders of apocryphal writings might not themselves be in this position but the authors and transmitters of the material most certainly are. Now it was about the time of the instruction to broadcast the 39th Festal Letter of Athanasius that someone or, what is more likely, a coterie decided to bury a large jar made of red slipware and of about 60 cm in height. Sealed by bitumen, the jar was probably to be the last home for 12 or 13 leather-bound books. The books contained 46 different texts together with duplicates of six of these. They were buried at the foot of a cliff eight kilometres west of the Pachomian monastery. Who buried them?

Athanasius we know was in hiding among the monks of Upper Egypt in AD 356 during a temporary 'turn-about' in his episcopal career. It was perhaps his observations while hiding there that furnished him with a view that 'some few of the simple should be beguiled from their simplicity and purity, by the subtlety of certain men, and should afterwards read other books – those called apocryphal'. Now, if these texts were buried in response to a heresy 'clearout' at the time of the broadcasting of the letter, then it was almost certainly the work of monks, in particular those monks who had most to lose from being associated with the condemned literature. If condemned as heretics, such people would suffer excommunication and the accompanying divorce from Christ's interests. Furthermore, the books would, according to practice, be burned. We are observing a stiffening in the regime governing the Coptic (that is, Egyptian) Church. Before this difficult period, it seems that in this area at least, orthodoxy coexisted with other types and tendencies of Christianity such as Jewish Christianity, a solitary and mystical ascetic Christianity and a now minority type of Christianity called Gnostic. If the buriers were from an orthodox monastery, fully coming to terms with the exclusive rigours of the Creed of Nicaea of AD 325 – which had been framed with the blessing of Athanasius – how is it that they would hold such books and where did they get them from?

In an interview with the current head of the Coptic Church, His Holiness Pope Shenouda gave a possible answer: 'As knowledge is spread everywhere, people try to have many books of knowledge. Whether from the Holy Bible or from philosophy or from any source of knowledge. And people had such books in their own libraries. Not because they were genuine gospels, but as books of knowledge. They may be considered books of literature, Coptic literature, not Coptic gospels.'

The careful burial of the books in the sand demonstrates a love and respect for their contents. It also indicates a tide of change sweeping through the monasteries towards a harder or more defined line on what the Christian must believe to be a Christian. Above all, it suggests a sadness at the passing of an era, from the time when a monk could truly escape from the world: a world where politics involved religion and religion would have to be shaped to fit in with political challenges. Athanasius would see this last phrase as inversely and perversely expressed: the Creed was for everyone. As we shall see, the books buried in the middle of the fourth century would not fit in with the Creed. They had to go.

As for those from whom the books originated, the books themselves show that they had already chosen not to 'fit in'. They were Gnostics – and they would have to go too.

This would not surprise them. They saw themselves as those who had both found and as those who sought a hidden truth, the very spirit of mystery. Rejecting all they had left behind, they and they alone were the advance guard of Humanity.

The Discovery

Beneath the sand, the jar was a kind of still womb. Inside the jar a small moment of history was silently hidden – unknown to the whole world. Empires will arise and decline, kings and queens will come and go, fashions will change, earth is ploughed and seeds are sown a thousand, thousand times. Blood is spilt, the sun shines, hopes appear and die again, an advance here, a retreat there. The texts lie silent in the unmoved air. Visions and prophets and sweat and toil. Struggles ensue: gunpowder, printing, voyages of discovery, genocide, inflation and fire; ages of reason, ages of faith, ages of magic, ages of war and ages of peace. The grains of sand are transplaced a million times. Far, far away: steam engines, electricity, blood and glory, monarchy and republic; riches and poverty, penicillin and gas; a million joys, a trillion tears; the telephone, the aeroplane and then, in August 1945 two atomic bombs fall on two cities in Japan.

How many times was it said that year that the 'sea shall give up her dead'? She does not always surrender to archaeologists, assorted salvage teams and bounty-hunters. Sometime in the December of 1945, three sons of ⸤Ali and ⸧Umm-Ahmad of the al-Sammān clan, Muḥammad, Khalifa and Abù al-Majd were out digging for *sabakh* with four camel-drivers not far from their home in al-Qaṣr, a village six kilometres from the town of Nag Hammadi on the main line to Cairo. *Sabakh* is birdlime and a good place to find it is beneath the high cliffs of the Jabal al-Tarīf, a kilometre away from the village of Hamra Dūm. It was near a large boulder, long since fallen from the cliff that the youngest brother, Abū, unearthed the jar. Muḥammad, who was ten years older, assumed the responsibility for dealing with the discovery.

Just over forty years later, Border Television's filmcrew were in the neighbourhood with Gilles Quispel, Professor of New Testament studies at the University of Utrecht, in order to film the location of the discovery. Our Production Manager, Valerie Kaye, was walking down the main street of al-Qaṣr with a copy of *Biblical Archaeologist* (Fall 1979) which featured a colour photograph of Muḥammad ʿAli al-Sammān on its cover. A rather serene-looking man in his mid-sixties walked up to her and, seeing the picture, pointed to it and then himself. He was the man responsible for discovering the Nag Hammadi Library.

This is how he tells the story:

> I found it at the Hamra Dūm mountain in the December of 1945. By 6 o'clock in the morning when I started my work ... all of a sudden I found this pot. And after I found it I had the feeling that there was something inside it. So I kept it, and because it was cold this morning ... I decided that I would leave it and would come back again for it to find out what's inside. I came back in the same day in fact, and I broke this pot. But I was afraid at the beginning because there might be something inside it – a jinn, a bad spirit. I was by myself when I broke the pot. I wanted my friends to be with me. After I broke it I found that it was a story book. I decided to bring my friends to tell them about the story. We were seven and we realized immediately that this has something to do with the Christian people. And we said that we don't really need it at all – it was just useless to us. So I took it to the ministry over here and he told me, well we really don't need it. It was just rubbish for us. So I took it back home. Some of them were burned and I tried to sell some of them.

Seven months before the discovery, Muḥammad ʿAli's father had been murdered. Suspicion in al-Qaṣr fell upon the son of the local sheriff: Aḥmad Ismāʿil of Hamra Dūm because the body of Muḥammad's father had been found near his home. Muḥammad's father, ʿAli Muḥammad Khalifa had been found shot in the head next to the decapitated body of what he, as a guard of irrigation machinery, had taken to be a thief from Hamra Dūm, the hamlet at the foot of the cliff where the discovery of the Nag Hammadi Library was to be made. It was Muḥammad ʿAli who had found his father's body and had thereupon, as is customary in these parts, sworn to avenge the murder of his beloved father.

Sometime between a few days and a month after the discovery of the

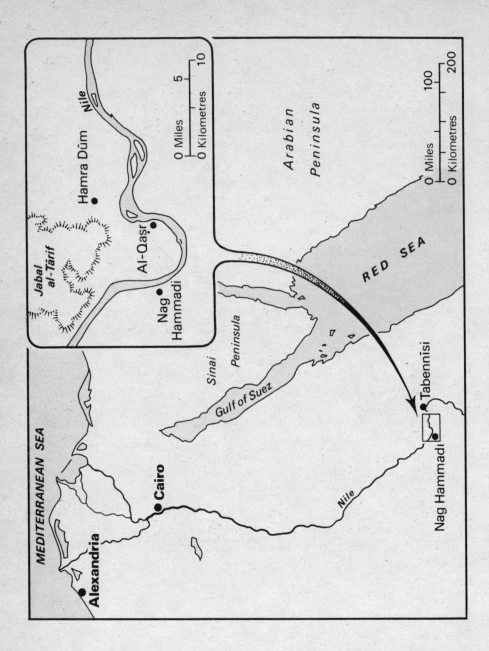

All that survives in stone which testifies to the gnostic presence in Rome: a memorial erected by the husband to his wife Flavia Sophē (see page 58). (From the National Museum of Rome)

jar, Aḥmad was seen sitting asleep by the road near Muḥammad ʿAli's home. On learning of this, ʿAli Muḥammad Khalifa's widow, armed her sons with sharpened mattocks and sent them to execute blood vengeance. They fell upon the victim and hacked Aḥmad to pieces, 'I took my knife and cut out his heart and ate most of his pieces.' A police investigation followed but none of the villagers of al-Qaṣr would come forward as witnesses because of widespread hatred of the sheriff from Hamra Dūm and fear of ʿAli's family. A short detention ensued for Muḥammad and his brothers but the crime went officially unsolved. The blood feud continues to this day.

'When I got out from the jail I found my mother had burned a lot of it and the only one which I really sold was for Mr Raghib. I got eleven [Egyptian] pounds for it.'

Did Muḥammad ʿAli know where the books were now?

'No, I have no idea.'

Did he have any regrets about the business?

'I don't care about it at all.'

Professor Quispel told him that he was a famous man and would be more famous still when the film of the proceedings was shown. Quispel continued, 'It is the first time that I come to Nag Hammadi, but I bought one of these books that you found. That was seven years since you discovered it. And ever since I have been working on it, and many other scholars have done too – owing to you. And your discovery will change the minds of millions. Well, so I'm very pleased to meet you.'

What happened to the Texts?

Had Muḥammad ʿAlī been able to read Coptic (that is, the ancient Egyptian language written in Greek letters), his eye might have strayed on to this passage in *Codex* (Book) *II*:

I shall give you what no eye has seen and what no ear has heard and what no hand has touched and what has never occurred to the human mind.

Or this one:

If they say to you, 'Where did you come from?', say to them, 'We came from the light, the place where the light came into being on its own accord and established [itself] and became manifest through their image.' If they say to you, 'Is it you?', say, 'We are its children, and we are the elect of the Living Father.' If they ask you, 'What is the sign of your Father in you?', say to them, 'It is movement and repose.'

Or:

Jesus said, 'Many times have you desired to hear these words which I am saying to you, and you have no one else to hear them from. There will be days when you will look for Me and will not find Me.'
Jesus said, 'It is I who am the light which is above them all. It is I who am the All. From Me did the All come forth, and unto Me did the All extend. Split a piece of wood, and I am there. Lift up the stone, and you will find Me there.'
And what is all this? 'These are the secret sayings which the living Jesus spoke and which Didymos Thomas wrote down.' And he said, 'Whoever finds the interpretation of these sayings will not experience death.'

Had Muḥammad ʿAlī not broken open the jar, we would not be able to hear these things. In the truest sense of the word, these things are dynamite. One might have imagined headlines throughout the world. Alas, these were only words, not gold. Publication of the Library did take a considerable amount of time. The above quotations (all from *The Gospel of Thomas* – the complete work unique to the library) were not published in English until 1959, while the entire library was not available in English until 1977, 32 years after the discovery. What took them so long?

For a start, the Library was very soon separated among Muḥammad ʿAli's friends and acquaintances in al-Qaṣr. Slowly, the papyrus codices began to turn up in Cairo having been obtained by various middle-men and antiquities dealers amid a certain amount of secrecy and rather shady deals with the original holders of the papyri.

On 4 October 1946, Togo Mina, the curator of the Coptic Museum in Cairo bought what is now *Codex III* for 250 Egyptian pounds from a Coptic (that is, Egyptian Christian) teacher from Nag Hammadi: Raghib Andarāwus 'al Quss' Abd as-Sajjid – the brother-in-law of the priest of al-Qaṣr and the man who claims to have been the first to recognize the antiquity of the library. *Codex III* contains the following works: *The Apocryphon* (Secret Book) *of John, The Gospel of the Egyptians, Eugnostos the Blessed, The Sophia of Jesus Christ* and *The Dialogue of the Saviour*.

Togo Mina alerted two French orientalists, Daumas and Corbin to the discovery, and they confirmed the Gnostic character of the Codex on the basis of a reading of *The Apocryphon of John*. Daumas returned to Paris and planned an edition for the following year. In September 1947, a young French scholar, Jean Doresse, went to Egypt and was there informed by Togo Mina of the discovery. He recognized the great importance of the Codex for our understanding of the origins of Christianity and he passed on the information to Étienne Drioton, Director of the Egyptian Department of Antiquities and to Henri-Charles Puech, an historian of religion based in Paris. It was about this time that business surrounding the texts began to take on an atmosphere that one might not expect from the apparently temperate world of international scholarship. Professor Elaine Pagels – a relatively late-comer to the field – has spoken of the 'dirty linen' of her profession, while Jean Doresse in his book *The Secret Books of the Egyptian Gnostics* (1958) wrote: 'If it were all to be gone through again, I confess that – although for my own part I received every possible assistance from the able scientific persons concerned, to whom I am profoundly grateful – I would probably think twice before I would again embroil myself for the sake of a discovery liable to arouse so many envies and jealousies.'

In December 1947, *Codex III* was put under glass for security. The announcement by Doresse to Togo Mina, that the discovery of the texts marked a new era in the study of Christian origins, encouraged Mina to show Doresse some papyrus leaves in the possession of Albert Eid, a

Belgian antiquities dealer. Togo Mina with his authority as curator of the Coptic Museum paid another visit to Eid in order to inform him that the papyri must never leave Egypt and must be sold to the Coptic Museum for a nominal price.

In 1948 the majority of the texts were still in private hands. Bahīj ᶜAli, the one-eyed contact in al-Qaṣr of the main middle-man, Zaki Basṭā, had obtained many texts. He went to Cairo to sell them. Phōcion Tano, a Cypriot antiquities dealer, bought all that he had (nine codices). Due to the uncertainty of laws regarding antiquity ownership, Tano was represented by the daughter of a noted Italian numismatist, Maria Dattari.

In October 1948, she, as 'owner' of the codices, contacted Doresse who made a survey of their contents. These included the jewel of the Library: *The Gospel of Thomas*. Doresse informed Drioton of what he had seen and advised purchase of the codices by the Coptic Museum. On reading in a French newspaper in Cairo that the Egyptian government was intervening to acquire the codices, Miss Dattari began a lawsuit which delayed research on the contents for three years. She eventually lost the lawsuit.

Meanwhile, Albert Eid, the Belgian antiquities dealer had been trying to elicit interest from the Bibliothèque Nationale in Paris, several university collections in the USA and the New York Bollingen Foundation. It appears that he met with almost total indifference. They did not want to know about Gnostic papyri. Having flown to the United States, and fearing a backlash should he return to Egypt, Albert Eid went directly to Belgium where he placed the Codex in a safe-deposit box, secured by a secret password. The year was 1949. On 17 June that year, Doresse gave a report on the Tano texts and *Codex III* to the Académie des Inscriptions et Belles-Lettres of the Institut de France in Paris. This was followed in 1950 by the first comprehensive survey of the discovery. Much credit therefore went to its author Henri-Charles Puech, Doresse's senior.

Enter Gilles Quispel: 'Well at that time I was a very young professor at the University of Utrecht, and I had already been trying to get hold of one of these manuscripts because I was especially interested in the gnostic Valentinus [more of him later]. And then I had the opportunity.' The Egyptian government had indicted Eid for smuggling antiquities but he died before a conviction could be made. Mrs Eid incurred a £6,000 fine on her husband's estate. The offending text was now in a Brussels bank and it was feared, by Quispel in particular, that the text might 'disappear' forever. Quispel had known of the attempt to sell the

Codex (now *Codex I* of the library) since the late 1940s and was now in a position, due to his scholarly interests and his friendship with the great Swiss psychologist Carl Gustav Jung, to take on the role of mediator in the purchase negotiations, pressing Jung as to the value of the Codex. Jung, at various times in his long career had shown a pronounced interest in what was then known of the Gnostics. Jung put his agent and associate, Doctor Meier, onto the matter. Meier located the owner and whereabouts of the text. Jung had some time since set up a foundation for the continuity and development of his analytical practice and psychological studies. This was the Bollingen Foundation, named after the lake by which Jung had personally built his home. In August 1951, the Bollingen Foundation agreed to purchase the Codex during the proceedings of the Jungian 'Eranos Conference' in Geneva.

Gilles Quispel fills in the story:

> Mr Meier had found out the address of the widow of the antiquity dealer who had brought it to the United States and there he went to the University of Michigan where they had a very famous collection of papyri. But there in America they said they had no money which meant that they despised gnosticism [a general term given by scholars to the beliefs and philosophy of, chiefly, the early 'Gnostics'] and didn't attach any importance to this collection. And the same happened to me, when I contacted the President of the Society for Scholarly Research in Holland, he said he had no time, which again (he was a theologian) meant that he didn't attach any importance to gnostic manuscripts. Jung, however, knew from his previous studies that gnosticism was very important and therefore contacted the Bollingen Foundation and asked them to finance the whole enterprise. At the last moment, the Bollingen Foundation couldn't do it because they were financing excavations in Egypt and therefore we were at a loss again – and at that decisive moment, Professor Meier contacted the American citizen Georgie Page, who lived in the neighbourhood of Zurich and he gave us 35,000 Swiss Francs and with this 35,000 Swiss Francs I went to Brussels on May 10th, 1952 and there I acquired the Codex you know, I gave a cheque of 35,000 francs, he [an unnamed agent of Mrs Eid] gave me the codex and with this codex under my arm, I returned home.

Codex I (the 'Jung Codex') remained in Quispel's study for a year and a half while he translated and studied it. When he had completed his first translation, he took it to show Jung at Lake Bollingen where Jung is quoted as having said: 'I have worked all my life to know the psyche – and these people knew already.' Quispel says, 'And it is true that *The Gospel of Truth* [the most important and most beautiful document in the Jung Codex] is such a vivid illustration of what man's predicament is according to Jung, that it could have been a falsification by a Jungian, which it is not!'

On 23 July 1952 the Egyptian monarchy collapsed in the Egyptian revolution. The texts in Egypt lay in the sealed box until autumn 1956. In the same year, the Coptic Gnostic Library was declared State property following the reorganization of the Department of Antiquities and the Coptic Museum under the direction of Pahor Labib. On 15 November 1953 there finally appeared a report on the purchase of the 'Jung Codex' by Puech and Quispel.

In 1955 came the first major description and more detailed account of *The Jung Codex. A Newly Recovered Gnostic Papyrus*. In the same year, Quispel was in Cairo negotiating the eventual return of the Codex to Egypt. (It was finally returned in 1975.) When Quispel arrived he was dismayed to find a proportion of the library – that which had been confiscated from Tano – still in a suitcase in the Director's office at the Coptic Museum. Quispel and Labib agreed that there should be an international committee of scholars established to undertake the complete translation and study of the library. The first result of this decision was a photographic copy of *The Gospel of Thomas* published by Pahor Labib. The year 1956 began well but ended badly for the project. Labib began with an inventory and glazing, aided by the Egyptian Coptologist Victor Girgis and the German, Martin Krause. It was discovered that there were only 11 complete codices out of a total of 12 or 13.

The Suez Crisis that year scuppered the progress of the international committee invited to Cairo for publication preparation. It was especially difficult for French scholars to gain access to Egypt due to the French political involvement with the attempted take-over of the Suez Canal. Gilles Quispel himself was happy to get out in time with the photographic copy of *The Gospel of Thomas* and his wife. He recalled, 'The American warship *Toban*, brought me from Alexandria to Naples. And I remember that there was a band playing on the quay that "Happy Days are Here Again!".'

Back in Europe *The Gospel of Truth* (published as *Evangelium Veritatis*) appeared in a sumptuous edition.

There was now something like a race going on as to who would put *The Gospel of Thomas* before the public first. For the English-speaking world the honours went to the editors and translators A. Guillaumont, Henri-Charles Puech, Gilles Quispel, W. Till and Y. 'Abd al Masih who published *The Gospel according to Thomas* in 1959. Doresse's book *The Secret Books of the Egyptian Gnostics* which included a translation of *The Gospel of Thomas* appeared in French in 1958.

Also in that year appeared the ripe fruits of over thirty years specialized scholarship, *The Gnostic Religion* by Professor Hans Jonas. Professor Jonas had completed his amazing survey of the Gnostic religion in 1954 without the benefit of the Nag Hammadi Library. Nevertheless, he could still assert in his Preface that, 'Our art and literature and much else would be different, had the gnostic message prevailed.'

So by the early 1960s there was sufficient heat in the academic air to promote a feeling, with some justification, that the world of scholarship was not only 'missing out' on something important but while being fed on what may perhaps have been morsels, a greater feast yet lay in store, indeed, was being denied to them. There was talk of a monopoly.

In 1961, the Director-General of UNESCO was alerted to the discovery by French scholars who urged publication of the entire find. They proposed another international committee. 'International' committees were now very much the order of the day. The Scandinavian archaeologist Torgny Sävy-Söderberg wrote to UNESCO speaking for himself and other scholars in urging the organization to intervene in order to prepare a complete edition of photographs of the texts so that the discovery might be placed at the disposal of disgruntled scholars internationally. This work was begun but was bogged down by incompetent preparation and various obstructions or scholars already working in Cairo.

In 1966 the Colloquium on the Origins of Gnosticism held at Messina took up an initiative to press ahead with the publication which had reached a standstill. On behalf of the Colloquium, Professor James M. Robinson, an American theologian took up the contact with UNESCO and his enthusiastic efforts, notwithstanding the six-day Arab–Israeli War, produced, in 1970, the Third International UNESCO Committee along with the Department of Antiquities of the Arab Republic of Egypt. This led directly to the inception of the publication of the Facsimile Edition of the Nag Hammadi Codices. In 1972 the first photographic edition was published, followed by nine other volumes and completed in 1977. Robinson and his team had privately circulated the material to scholars throughout the world and their combined efforts also gave the public *The Nag Hammadi Library in English* published by E. J. Brill of Leiden under the editorship of James M. Robinson. In the Introduction, Robinson wrote that, 'Now the time has come for a concentrated effort, with the whole Nag Hammadi Library accessible, to rewrite the history of Gnosticism, to understand what it was really all about, and of course to pose new questions. Rarely has a generation of students had such an opportunity!'

Quite so – and neither has the general public!

The Texts

In 1977, when the Nag Hammadi Library was first published, I took my entrance examinations for Oxford University where I intended to study Theology. It was also in that year that I made a design for a poster which featured the words, 'Creation is the Product of Pain' – over which I placed a crucifix. The constant refrain of my thoughts before sleep was 'Time must stop. I must transcend time.' I did not then know that such thoughts belong to a long but frequently broken 'tradition' which I have now come to term gnostic.

My sources, insofar as I was aware of them, were those strains of Platonist philosophy as expressed by the English poets, George Herbert, William Blake and Samuel Taylor Coleridge. It would be some years before I discovered their sources and describe them as a diluted gnosis, moulded to an English experience.

Eighteen months later I read of the Nag Hammadi Discovery while studying for a routine Oxford essay on 'Gnosticism'. The 'official' view held that Gnosticism was a Christian heresy based upon a travesty of Christian doctrine, corrupted by magic, loaded by an impossible weight of mythology and crazy thinking which would lead to an abyss where 'salvation' was lost. I remember writing that the Gnostic myths could be seen as a kind of 'map' of the mind's experience as it searches for the root of itself and its meaning – those things which could only be expressed in richly imaginative terms, those things for which the heart has reasons the reason knows not of. But what of the texts themselves? What are they really about? Why did scholars get so excited about them?

Firstly, one must say that they were new texts. Of the 51 texts 41 were previously unknown. Here was an opportunity to make a scholar's reputation. If one looks at the Bible, there are thousands of books available on any single component. The work has become more and more refined and it is unlikely that any new work on the Bible will be greeted with amazement. However, a first work on a new text will become, no matter how the study develops and contradicts the original study, a standard reference point: a place in the history books. Having said this, one must consider that these were 'Gnostic' works and this suggests a secret Knowledge demanding a high attainment of intellect together with an irresistible aura of mystery. There is a strong romantic pull at work here.

Thirdly, there is the lure of the Unknown. Gnostic thought was markedly different to orthodox thought – one might discover genuinely new insights into the human condition. After all, who knows what answers to perennial questions still lie beneath the sea or sand? Answers given at the time the questions were put. One might contact the original, untarnished thought-processes of a portion of mankind. One might penetrate the haze of twentieth-century know-all *ennui* and reach out to a brighter era enlightened by ancient clarity. There already existed a precedent. The Renaissance had largely consisted of just this process: ancient learning giving birth to a fresh creative impulse. One might live again.

The 51 texts were bound in books which contained between two and eight works. They were made of papyrus, that is to say that strips of the fibrous pith which the stalks of the papyrus plant contained were peeled off and placed side by side. These were then covered with a second layer at right angles to the first. The result was then pressed and dried, making for a long-lasting, smooth writing surface. These strips were usually about 20 cm in length but some of those used in the Nag Hammadi Library were over a metre in length. This has been considered to be something of a technological feat for the time and might evince to the importance of the text for those who had them made. These surfaces were in turn placed next to each other and pasted together to form a papyrus roll of about 3 metres in length. This roll was then divided into strips of between 20 and 40 cm in width. When one had between twenty and forty of these, they were gathered together and folded down the middle. The result was a book. You could write on both sides of the paper and you were saved the inconvenience and wear and tear which went with the 'roll' or 'scroll' format. The book format was an innovation of the first centuries of our era and the Nag Hammadi Library is the largest early collection of such books or codices from the latin *codex*: the forerunner of the book being a set of waxed wooden tablets tied together. The papyri were held together in leather stiffened with 'used' papyrus while the tail of the animal skin was attached to a thong which was wrapped around the finished codex. The covers were tooled in a simple way and some of them include crosses. In *Codex III* there is a note made by the scribe which says that 'in the flesh my name is Gongessos'. He also had a spiritual name, Eugnostos, and refers to his 'fellow lights in incorruptibility'. He describes the text as 'God-written',

Concerning the date of composition (of the Codices – not their sources), fragments of letters and receipts used to reinforce the bindings give us some clues. Two receipts bear the dates 333, 341, 346 and 348. We can use this information together with a study of the kind of writing employed to arrive at a date of about AD 350. The compound of the ink employed contained soot and the contrast between this and the sometimes light golden hue of the papyrus has produced some texts of great beauty – *The Gospel of Truth* can be especially cited. But what does the writing say?

First of all the language employed is Coptic which was the spoken language of the Egyptians written mainly in Greek letters. A study of the language has shown that many of the works are translations from the Greek. So what we do not find in the main are writings about Egyptian religion – although there are some notable exceptions. What we do find, however, is a collection of writings which, though differing widely in content and understanding, share a pervading feeling, a philosophical feeling concerned chiefly with certain kinds of religious experience. In *Codex II* there is a work entitled *The Gospel of Philip* in which a reference is made to an independent tradition about Jesus – independent that is from the Catholic tradition which informs the structure and content of the New Testament:

> He said on that day in the Thanksgiving, 'You have joined the perfect, the light, with the Holy Spirit, unite the angels with us also, the images.'

In the same gospel it is said:

> When a blind man and one who sees are both together in darkness, they are no different from one another. When the light comes, then he who sees will see the light, and he who is blind will remain in darkness.

We have all heard of, and probably used the expression 'He or she has seen the light'. We may say this in a banal way or we may say it with seriousness and, not uncommonly, with a good deal of relief as well! We don't mean that the person has seen something, 'a light', with their eyes, outside of themselves. We mean that, perhaps quite suddenly, a person sees more of his or her situation than before, as though the shutters in a room one thought was small and perpetually dark were opened, without our having done anything, and then one sees that it is a large room and quite beautiful too – a little cleaning here and there might be required – but, well, what a room! How could I have been *so* blind? We all know the story of Scrooge on Christmas morning. He has *seen*, really seen in a visionary way what had always been before his eyes, namely, that he was a greedy selfish old man. He was transformed and he transformed all those who saw him on that Christmas morning. 'There is light within a man of light, and he lights up the whole world. If he does not shine, he is darkness,' says the Jesus of *The Gospel of*

Thomas. Now what marks the authors of these works apart is precisely this: that they all hold the vision of the 'light' to be the central principle of life. It must have been a very special experience of the light which made them think in the ways they did:

> Do not make the kingdom of heaven a desert within you. Do not be proud because of the light that illumines, but be to yourselves as I myself am to you. For your sakes I have placed myself under the curse, that you may be saved.
>
> (from *The Apocryphon of James*)

> For when they had seen him and had heard him, he granted them to taste him and to smell him and to touch the beloved Son. When he had appeared instructing them about the Father, the incomprehensible one, when he had breathed into them what is in the mind, doing his will, when many had received the light, they turned to him. For the material ones were strangers and did not see his likeness and had not known him. Again, speaking new things, still speaking about what is in the heart of the Father, he brought forth the flawless word.
>
> (from *The Gospel of Truth*)

What is this 'light'?

> I am the light which exists in the light, I am the remembrance of the Providence – that I might enter into the middle of darkness and the inside of Hades.
>
> (from *The Apocryphon of John*)

> The kingdom of the Father is spread out upon the earth, and men do not see it.
>
> (from *The Gospel of Thomas*)

Men do not see it. A Gnostic however had most definitely seen the 'Light'. If we return for a moment to the analogy of the darkened room. For the Gnostic, the darkened room is the world – the 'world' of man's experience without the 'Light'. The nature of *this* world is dark and heavy. It changes and is full of uncertainty. It is a world of gross matter, subject to decay and death. It is a theatre of war, of domination and destruction. It is a world full of illusions, of false promises and pain. It is a world where men and women go hungry while animals consume each other. It is a world in which movement is forced. It is characterized by fatigue and distress. It is, in short, a *material* world.

Now we can come to the root of the matter. What the Gnostic knows (and the word gnostic means a 'knower') is that this world, as I have described it, is not his or her true home. While the world sleeps the Gnostic awakes:

He who hears, let him get up from the deep sleep. Arise and remember that it is you who hearkened, and follow your root, which is I, the merciful one.

(from *The Apocryphon of John*)

I tell you this that you may know yourself.

(from *The Apocryphon of James*)

At the very heart, at the 'root' of the Gnostic is the 'living Jesus'. This is what it means to 'know yourself'. The Gnostic knows that he or she is a spiritual being, 'of one substance with the Father'; for what the orthodox say of Christ, the Gnostic is free to say of himself. They do not believe they have denigrated Jesus but that they have discovered the proper dignity of Man: to be an elevated being is what being a Gnostic is all about. He will 'be like a tree growing by a meandering stream'. He will be in the 'Light' and in his spiritual being he will have wings:

Everyone who seeks the truth from true wisdom will make himself wings so as to fly, fleeing the lust that scorches the spirits of men.

(from *The Book of Thomas the Contender*)

The Gnostic feels intensely his freedom from the world:

Whoever has come to understand the world has found a corpse, and whoever has found a corpse is superior to the world.

(from *The Gospel of Thomas*)

The Gnostic clearly distinguished himself from the great mass of human beings who did not share this experience: 'They have always been attracted downwards' (*Book of Thomas the Contender*). Such people were described as 'hylic', that is 'material'. This means that there is none of that divine light within them which longs for union with the Father. It is the guiding dynamic of gnostic thought that divine light has become imprisoned within the material world and must be returned:

Hasten to be saved without being urged. And, if possible arrive even before me – for thus the Father will love you.

(from *The Apocryphon of James*)

To have the gnosis (knowledge of where one comes from, into what one has been thrown and where one is going) is to become part of the great cosmic rescue plan. The aim of the rescue plan is to heal the original divine being (called the Pleroma, that is, Fullness) which has tragically given birth to a deficient creation:

For the knowledge of the things which are ordained is truly the healing of the passions of matter.

(from Asclepius)

In the *Apocryphon of John* the Gnostic Jesus says, 'I am the remembrance of the Pleroma.' Remembrance. There has occurred a kind of cosmic amnesia. People do not know where they come from. Most of mankind does not seem to care. For those who do, they begin to yearn; they begin to suffer and then, if they listen to their deepest heart, from out of the Fullness of Being (the Pleroma) their cry is heard by the Father who sends his Son, the saviour Jesus to rescue the lonely soul. The voice of the saviour is familiar. It is a remembrance, an awakening. There is joy and a profound knowing:

> Blessed are the solitary and elect, for you will find the kingdom. For you are from it, and to it you will return.

(from The Gospel of Thomas)

The gnostic Jesus comes from the spiritual world within and above, appearing to those who are awake. To those who are not, who do not have the gnosis, He is merely an image made of flesh. Flesh of itself is without life. It is part of the world. To the Gnostic, the world of material perception has become an image and is no longer subject to its control:

> You walked in mud,
> and your garments were not soiled,
> and you have not been buried in their filth,
> and you have not been caught.
> (from the *First Apocalypse of James*)

Before leaving the world of matter, Jesus says this to his disciples:

> Watch and pray that you not come to be in the flesh, but rather that you come forth from the bondage of the bitterness of this life. And as you pray, you will find rest, for you have left behind the suffering and the disgrace. For when you come forth from the sufferings and passion of the body, you will receive rest from the Good one, and you will reign with the King, you joined with him and he with you, from now on, for ever and ever. Amen.

(from The Book of Thomas the Contender)

I hope that what has preceded gives the reader some idea of the world of feeling, thought and experience which informs a good deal of the Nag Hammadi Library. To talk of the 'message' of the Library would be unwise. The Library is not to be seen, as some see the Bible, as a big homogenous lump of Truth. There are books in the Library which seem to be exclusively concerned with exclusivity – identifying the authors and those 'in the know' to which they are addressed as the only wise, and all others as fools fit for grinding. Some of the works take a radical view which holds that the world we live in is wholly evil and who seem to be ignorant of those lines of thought and understanding which see the kingdom of heaven spread out upon the world but yet unseen. I think the reader today is in a position to take in what appears to make sense and reject what is apparently silly or incomprehensible. It was surely the practice of the original holders of the texts to keep books which in the main may have been disagreeable in the knowledge that some kernel of insight here or there mediated on their behalf and so made the text worthy of preservation. It accords with what we know of the gnostic mind to think that they may have realized that what appeared to be insensible may in time yield an understanding for which they were not yet ready.

This necessary reserve brings us to the last major question which needs to be addressed on the subject of the Library and one which may be of most significance to some readers.

Did God write the Nag Hammadi Library?

We have seen from the preceding discourse that the Gnostic felt removed from ordinary perception. These books were the records of outsiders, of aliens. Indeed, one of the books is entitled *Allogenes* which is translated as 'of another race' or 'stranger' or 'alien'. Their experience of the world as they thought and felt it, was fundamentally different to the rest of humanity. Insofar as the world which exists for each one of us is the world as we perceive it in our minds, the Gnostic lived in a different world. They believed that their perception and experience was timeless – outside of the conditions of time and space. They sometimes refer to themselves as the 'immovable ones'. They felt that they were not, in their essential being, subject to the laws and conditions which govern life on earth. This being, this self beyond the world, was only temporarily attached to the gross body: 'The Living are not affected by anything except the state of being in the flesh alone, which they bear while looking expectantly for the time when they will be met by the receivers' (from the *Apocryphon of John*).

This extraordinary awareness, this gnosis, this ability to move from terra firma to the source of that 'Light' which they believed illumined them, this familiarity with the 'Living Jesus' gave them, we might say naturally gave them, a privileged access to the outflow of the divine mind. Thus, our scribe, Gongessos can say that his work is 'God-written'. It has been written by one who has, as it were, broken through the images that are visible in the material world to the invisible, spiritual world that the Gnostic might believe to be 'behind' them. For the Gnostic, this constituted authority enough. On the other hand, there was a tolerance within the Gnosis of the value of the subjective experience. This is to say that the Gnostic could say, well, that is your vision of things but it is not the same as mine and I cannot believe your vision has any authority over mine unless I experience it for myself. This view was also taken with regard to the New Testament, that 'Canon, accredited as Divine' which Athanasius says in the 39th Festal Letter is the yardstick and substance of authoritative Catholic scripture. By 'Catholic' I mean 'what is held universally in the universal church'. The Gnostic asks, 'What does it mean when Christ says in *The Gospel of John*, "I am the Door"?' He might then meditate upon this and achieve what he is convinced is a communication from the 'Living Jesus' who tells him that it means, 'Knock on yourself as upon a door.' Which, one may ask, is the truly and divinely inspired scripture? The orthodox answer is 'that which is held universally by the Church and is in accordance with the tradition of the teaching of the apostles'. But the Gnostic is not concerned with the universal Church – he has a universe within himself. He believes he is going right to the source and is wary that the Church is becoming or has become a middle-man with special interests of its own, namely, the continuity of the Church structure. Again, we see a clash of world experiences. Of course, we are in a position today to justifiably question or disbelieve in any such thing as 'divinely inspired scripture'.

The use of the predicate 'Living' when attached to Jesus does suggest that the authors are aware of a distinction between the Jesus who walked around Palestine and the eternal figure of Jesus who is able to appear as 'Light' before Paul on his way to Damascus. Many Christians today say that they talk with Jesus and that he gives them verbal guidance. But they do not print up their dialogues. I think this is important. It tells us something about the way Jesus is regarded. For the person referred to, such communication with Christ is personal, concerning matters of this life and not really communicable to another. It is a private matter, the substance of prayer. The Gnostic, however, regarded Jesus as being unconcerned with the affairs of this world unless they had a directly spiritual bearing. So what Jesus – and it is not always Jesus who is the communicator from the divine world in the Nag

Hammadi Library – what the spiritual being has to offer is information about the spiritual world and what those principles are which provide access to it: frequently occult or 'hidden' knowledge. This information was of interest to some Gnostics. Having begun with an experience of gnosis, of knowledge, the Gnostic would soon become aware that there was yet more to know. In fact, there was no end to knowledge and no limits to the fathoming of the divine being – the inner being of the Gnostic. Each new item of information would thus make the previous one obsolete – but it might still be useful for another Gnostic who was on the road to 'home'. Hence, we find many of the books in the Library listing now (and possibly then) incomprehensible names of the spiritual beings one might encounter on the inner journey to the Pleroma. The books *Allogenes, The Nature of the Archons, On the Origin of the World, The Book of Thomas the Contender, The Gospel of the Egyptians, Eugnostos, the Blessed, The Apocalyspe of Adam, The Thunder: Perfect Mind, The Concept of Our Great Power, The Dialogue on the Eighth and Ninth, The Paraphrase of Shem, The Three Steles of Seth, Zostrianos, Marsanes* and *Trimorphic Protennoia* all share elements of these features. Indeed, one might say of the Library that the more eccentric sounding the title is to English ears the more the work is likely to be concerned with this gnostic attitude of getting information about 'realities behind appearances' from inner contemplation in those states of mind to which a gnostic experience might have provided entry. As to the origin of the ideas, language and message of such works, one is, as the Gnostic was, at liberty to speculate. Speculation is not, however, what most people want from a religion which is offering salvation. The Catholic Church felt acutely the necessity of establishing a body of scripture which, while providing for the philosophers a basis for speculation, was stable and universally accepted – and accessible to a body of worshippers and not only to an individual.

What we really want to know is of course the answer to the question: did Jesus of Nazareth ever say, in his lifetime on earth, any of the things put into his mouth in the gnostic texts? Is there a reliable tradition here of Jesus's sayings while in the flesh? Was Jesus's 'real' message a gnostic one? With regard to the question about the nature of Jesus's message – was it a gnostic one? – I think that an incident in my life may provide a clue. I know a Sikh Rajinder Nijjhar, who, with characteristic Indian boldness, informed me that, 'You cannot read the New Testament unless you are gnostic.' He means that the words of the New Testament will not yield their full meaning unless one gains access to the spirit in which the words were formed, unless one had the gnosis in fact. It is a characteristic of the gnostic attitude to an inspired text to believe that it has an outer sense – for ordinary 'faithful' people – and an inner sense whose dimensions of meaning may be endless. This experience is, of course, akin to that of many people who would deny that their attitude was gnostic. The genuine Gnostic would believe that he had broken into or rather had been permitted to enter the secret world of spirit from which the words came and, most importantly, that same world from which he derived. This gave the Gnostic 'pneumatic' (that is, spiritual one) the power to interpret scripture according to his own experience of the divine and, furthermore, to add to scripture by virtue of the divine origins he shared with the revealer of gnosis. For Christian gnostics, Jesus existed within the Gnostic's own being while his own being existed within the 'Light'. He was a child of the 'Light', and consequently in potential or in fact was divine. The Christian Gnostic believed that Jesus had revealed the Gnostic's true self and that was 'the root, which is I, the merciful one'. In short, in answer to the question, 'Was Jesus's message gnostic?' The answer is, 'Yes, if you are a Gnostic.'

Some of the most interesting examples of this gnostic approach to scripture can be found in the way two documents of the 'Nag Hammadi Library' deal with the crucifixion.

In the work *The Second Treatise to the Great Seth*, Jesus Christ in a revelation to a group of gnostic disciples tells them the real story,

> For my death which they think happened, happened to them in their error and blindness, since they nailed their man unto their death.
> It was another upon whom they placed the crown of thorns. But I was rejoicing in the height over all the wealth of the archons and the offspring of their error, of their empty glory. And I was laughing at their ignorance.

The author is saying that the spiritual Jesus has appeared to him in his 'real' form – as a spiritual being in order to explain the 'appearance' of the crucifixion. He is saying in effect, 'You have read how in the New Testament that I was beaten and humiliated and then crucified. Well, it only looked that way – and the writers of the New Testament, to them it was given in the material sense. But to you, who have come to understand and see the spiritual world, the real world beyond the appearances, I can tell you what was really happening. The body, what appeared to be my body belongs to the world of flesh. The world of flesh and matter is governed by the archons (that is rulers, invisible to men and ignorant of the true Father, dedicated to keeping man on the material plain, subjecting man to law and bondage) and they tried to have power over me as they have power over the rest of the world. But at the moment when they thought they had triumphed over me, I was released from the body and watched them from above. And I could really see what was going on and they couldn't see me – you should have seen them in their blindness! So while it looked to you that it was a wicked day, it was really a day a triumph! You too can laugh at the archons because they can only get your body. They cannot kill the real you!'

This reality behind appearance is the gospel, the 'good news' for the Gnostic. Another gnostic author, this time of *The Apocalypse of Peter*, tells the story rather differently. This the Gnostic felt at liberty to do – originality was the sign that the Gnostic had the special creative insight of gnosis. History, as we understand it, was of no interest to them. It was not a question of, 'what was the event?' but of 'what does this mean to me?' In *The Apocalypse of Peter* the identity of the author is subsumed beneath the identity of Peter. The author imagines himself as Peter. For the author, Peter is not an historical person here but expresses a relationship of closeness to the Saviour. He puts Peter in the Temple in Jerusalem, that is, he puts himself there, talking to the Saviour, trying to understand how Jesus would respond to the developments of the Church and the Church's understanding of him. There, in the imaginative freedom of the spirit, Peter has a vision:

I saw him seemingly being seized by them. And I said, 'What do I see, O Lord, that it is you yourself whom they take, and that you are grasping me? Or who is this one, glad and laughing on the tree? And is it another one those feet and hands they are striking?'

The Saviour said to me, 'He whom you saw on the tree, glad and laughing, this is the living Jesus. But this one into whose hands and feet they drive the nails is his fleshly part, which is the substitute being put to shame, the one who came into being in his likeness. But look at him and me.'

But I, when I had looked, said, 'Lord, no one is looking at you. Let us flee this place.'

But he said to me, 'I have told you, "Leave the blind alone!" And you, see how they do not know what they are saying. For the son of their glory instead of my servant they have put to shame.'

And I saw someone about to approach us resembling him, even him who was laughing on the tree. And he was (filled) with a Holy Spirit, and he is the Saviour. And there was a great, ineffable light around them, and the multitude of ineffable and invisible angels blessing them. And when I looked at him, the one who gives praise was revealed.

Through this vision the author saw himself. Who is to say that he was misled? Were the Gnostics of the Nag Hammadi Library then what we might call 'dreamers', offering imagined solutions to perennial questions?

Was the Gnosis a collection of 'fantasies'? I do not believe it is possible to give definitive answers to these questions. Much lies in the 'eyes of the beholder'. Much has been learned in the twentieth century about the importance of dream. Some go to a modern art gallery and see riches glorious while others see an incomprehensible mess; others still desire to apply rules to what they see in order to subdivide the artwork and provide solace for the two sides – and themselves. Now while it may be that the vast majority of books in the Nag Hammadi collection are specialized and rebellious offshoots of early Christianity, post-dating the composition of books of the New Testament from between about fifty to 280 years, there are reasons to believe that the Gnosis, as a religious concept of itself, goes back in less developed forms to the time of Christ and possibly earlier than that. Several works sharing the titles of those in the Nag Hammadi Library are referred to in the second century. In about AD 180, Bishop Irenaeus of Lyon, mentions a *Gospel of Truth* and a *Secret Book of John*, while in the third century, the great philosopher Plotinus's pupil Porphyry mentions (with some disgust) works called *Allogenes* and *Zostrianos*. Several of the works bear the imprints of the 'mind' of the followers of Valentinus, the greatest gnostic teacher who was active in Rome (and nearly became bishop) around AD 160 and whose influence and fame lasted for at least 300 years after that. It is thought that the remarkable *Gospel of Truth* may very well have come from his pen.

However, the one book which has the greatest claim to primacy (if we accept that what is earliest is also most likely to be most pure and possibly true) in the matter of its date of composition is without doubt *The Gospel of Thomas. The Gospel* begins:

These are the hidden words which the living Jesus spoke and Didymos, Judas Thomas wrote down and he said, 'Whoever will find the interpretation of these sayings will not experience death.'

Here Gilles Quispel describes the first time he read these words:

... in the fall of 1956. When I was sitting here [in Cairo] in a hotel in the evening near the Metropolitan Museum, and trying to translate them from a photocopy. And it was an experience to have before you a text that you don't understand at all, and bring these characters together and relay them to history. And every time there was 'Jesus said', 'Jesus said'. Then in the back of your mind you have always the idea; can that be an unknown and yet authentic word of Jesus. Because in almost 2,000 years of Christian tradition, never a collection of unknown sayings has been discovered. So it was an enormous experience. Very exciting, and well, it took me the rest of my years to prove that my original intuition was right. That we had here an independent tradition of the sayings of Jesus.

Do these sayings belong in the Bible?

Well, I'm not a prince of the Church, I'm not a bishop or a Pope, and these are the people that determine the Canon. But according to a considered opinion of scholars that have seriously studied *The Gospel of Thomas*, some of these sayings are nearer to the source than the sayings of Jesus transmitted in the canonical gospels.

In a book published in 1962 *Thomas and the Evangelists* by H.E.W. Turner and Hugh Montefiore (formerly the Bishop of Birmingham) it is concluded:

It is therefore fair to conclude that despite the form in which it is cast and for all its impressive indebtedness to the canonical tradition, the thought climate of the document is alien to the world of the New Testament. *The Gospel of Thomas* may have appeared to its compiler 'the secret words which Jesus the Living One spake'; despite the claims of the rest of the Preamble they are not, for those who take the New Testament as their guide, the words of eternal life.

So it was a thumbs-down from the Church of England anyway.

The Gospel of Thomas does contain sayings of Jesus which appear in the canonical gospels, Luke and Matthew. This was of interest to scholars who have long held a sayings-source called 'Q' (from the German *Quelle* meaning Source) to have been employed by those gospel writers in conjuction with Mark. It is possible that *The Gospel of Thomas* was another sayings-source circulating in the Jewish Christian church in Syria before the composition of Luke and Matthew (*circa* AD 70–90). Luke, who represents much of the New Testament 'thought climate' begins his gospel with the statement: 'Forasmuch as many have taken in hand to draw up a narrative of those matters which have been fulfilled among us ... '. Luke does not say that these other narratives, of which he says there are many, were 'apocryphal' and unacceptable to the Church. By the time of Athanasius's 39th Festal Letter, it was long established that there were only four gospels which revealed divinely inspired truth. Athanasius even paraphrases Luke's form of words saying, 'Forasmuch as some have taken in hand, to reduce into order for themselves the books termed apocryphal ... '.

Having said this, it is important to recall those passages in the New Testament which speak of things which are not written within it. The most obvious passage is that of Mark IV. 10–12 which has often perplexed readers but perhaps makes more sense from a gnostic perspective:

> And when he was alone, they that were about him with the twelve asked of him the parables.
>
> And he said unto them, Unto you is given the mystery of the kingdom of God: but unto them that are without, all things are done in parables:
>
> That seeing they may see, and not perceive; and hearing they may hear, and not understand; lest haply they should turn again, and it should be forgiven them.

A very mysterious passage indeed and in all my reading I have never found a satisfactory explanation of it. It is this very mystery which appeals to the gnostic mind, drawing him in as a fish in a net ... Saint Paul too is aware of the mysteries but he is also aware, deeply aware of the spiritual pride, the inflation of the ego which experience of the mysteries may lead to. He speaks about this in his second letter to the Corinthians. Many scholars believe that Paul came up against a gnostic tendency in Corinth which threatened to split the young church on the familiar basis of the gnostic distinction between the simple faithful and the more 'enlightened' spiritual consciousness. Paul saw the issue as one of pride and says in the wonderful passage in I Corinthians XIII that it is Love that matters most of all, that the loving heart is dearer to God than the wisest of wise sayings. Nevertheless, one senses that Paul has been deeply disquieted by the experience of a gnosis of Christ which has the power to divide the followers of Christ. He writes in II Corinthians XII. 1–7:

> I must needs glory, though it is not expedient; but I will come to visions and revelations of the Lord. I know a man in Christ [usually thought to be Paul himself] fourteen years ago (whether in the body, I know not; or whether out of the body, I know not; God knoweth), such a one caught up even to the third heaven. And I know such a man (whether in the body, or apart from the body, I know not; God knoweth), How that he was caught up into Paradise, and heard unspeakable words, which it is not lawful for a man to utter. On behalf of such a one will I glory: but on mine own behalf I will not glory, save in my weaknesses. For if I should desire to glory, I shall not be foolish; for I shall speak the truth: but I forbear, lest any man should account of me above that which he seeth me to be, or heareth from me. And by reason of the exceeding greatness of the revelations – wherefore, that I should not be exalted

overmuch, there was given to me a thorn in the flesh, a messenger of Satan to buffet me, that I should not be exalted overmuch.

Paul is saying, 'I know what you people are talking about. I've been there and I know the temptation to glorify myself. But the experience has humbled me and I would rather glorify the vision of another.' It would not be long before the visionary would become suspect in the Church and a substantial part of the spiritual gifts which Paul's churches enjoyed would be downgraded, and, in the case of the Gnosis, excluded altogether.

Just how and why this happened will be set forth in the next two chapters. But before we leave the Nag Hammadi Library for a while, look again at the mysterious (to me at least) Chapter IV of Mark's gospel, verses 19 and 21–22:

And the cares of the world, and the deceitfulness of riches, and the lusts of other things entering in, choke the word, and it becometh unfruitful.

And he said unto them, Is the lamp brought to be put under the bushel, or under the bed, and not to be put on the stand?

For there is nothing hid, save that it should be manifested; neither was anything made secret, but that it should come to light.

and see what the Gnostic makes of this theme in *The Gospel of Thomas*:

Businessmen and merchants will not enter the Places of my Father.

Recognise what is in your sight and that which is hidden from you will become plain to you. For there is nothing hidden which will not become manifest.

The images are manifest to men, but the light in them remains concealed in the image of the light of the Father. He will become manifest, but his image will remain concealed by his light.

I think that modern man can only accept what he experiences and he can see, he can learn from the Gnostics that he can experience much more than he is aware of. And therefore I think that for both true believers and unbelievers, gnosis is very important, because it will reveal to them an unknown dimension within themselves.

(Professor Gilles Quispel. Cairo, Spring 1986).

Chapter Two

The Higher Reason

Βασιλευς ὁ Νους
The Higher Reason is king
(Plotinus. b. AD 204)

Rome *circa* AD 150. An Egyptian poet is writing a book. He gazes into the dark heart of the Empire and sees:

terror and disturbance and instability and doubt and division, there were many illusions at work by means of these, and there were empty fictions, as if they were sunk in sleep and found themselves in disturbing dreams. Either there is a place to which they are fleeing, or without strength they come from having chased after others, or they are involved in striking blows, or they are receiving blows themselves, or they have fallen from high places, or they take off into the air though they do not even have wings. Again, sometimes it is as if people were murdering them, though there is no one even pursuing them, or they themselves are killing their neighbours, for they have been stained with their blood. When those who are going through all these things wake up, they see nothing, they who were in the midst of all these disturbances, for they are nothing. Such is the way of those who have cast ignorance aside from them like sleep, not esteeming it as anything, nor do they esteem its works as solid things either, but they leave them behind like a dream in the night. The knowledge of the Father they value as the dawn. This is the way each one has acted, as though asleep at the time when he was ignorant. And this is the way he has come to knowledge, as if he had awakened.

The poet is almost certainly the Christian Gnostic Valentinus who we know was in Rome from AD 135–160, during the heyday of Gnosis.

At about the same time as the poet was writing this terrifying and perhaps familiar account of the rootless soul coming to consciousness, another writer, Apuleius, a pagan from Madaura (a Roman colony in North Africa), was writing a work on the philosophy of Plato. In it, the writer is keen to stress the sense of stability and permanence of ultimate realities. The reader is to distinguish between that which changes and is sensible to touch and that which is intelligible, that is, perceived consistently by the 'noetic', the *nous*, the intuitive faculty – the higher reason.

> There are also two natures [or essences] of things. And of these, one pertains to things which may be seen by the eyes, and touched by the hand, and which Plato calls doxastic [or the subject of opinion]; but the other is the object of intellect and is dianöetic and intelligible. For pardon must be granted to novelty of words, when it serves to illustrate the obscurity of things. And the former nature is indeed mutable and easily to be perceived; but the latter, which is seen by the piercing eye of intellect, and is known and conceived by the acute energy of the reasoning power, is incorruptible, immutable, stable, and invariably and perpetually the same.
>
> Hence, also, he says, That there is a twofold method of interpretation [pertaining to them]. For that visible nature is known by a fortuitous suspicion, and which is of no long duration; but this intelligible essence is demonstrated to exist, by true, perpetual, and stable reasoning. But time is the image of eternity; since time is moved, but the nature of eternity is firm and immovable.

Both Valentinus and Apuleius are deeply concerned with finding a point of stability in an uncertain and changing world. For Valentinus, that point emerges as the gnosis (knowledge) of who one is, where one comes from and into what one has appeared and awakened to. The Gnostic, while before gnosis felt alienated, now after gnosis, knows he is alien but the knowledge no longer causes anguish and misery but a sense of freedom and peace or 'movement and repose': 'The knowledge of the Father they value as the dawn' (*Gospel of Truth*). The Gnostic has emerged from the nightmare of unconscious existence as a profoundly changed person: he knows that at the very ground of his being, at his root, is the Father – 'the primal-incomprehensible'. Incomprehensible no doubt, but when we have faith in a person and we say we 'know' them – that does not mean that we understand them intellectually. Many in our times, following an intellectual psychology as a path to self-knowledge have often found that it fails to make them really understand the people they are living with and does not really help those other people to understand them. The Gnostic has made contact with eternity – the fullness and love of the eternal Father of All – what more could there possibly be to worry about?

What to some extent, the Gnostic has attained to by the experience of gnosis, the philosopher sees by the 'piercing eye of intellect'. By intellect, Apuleius does not mean what passes for the intellect today, that is, the abstract binding power of reason – that which binds ideas in coherent patterns and assigns measure and proportion to them. Apuleius means something operating by the energy of intelligence – it is a light one sometimes sees in the gardener's or craftsman's eye when he or she comes to approach the very substance of their labours – the meaning of their contact with nature. It is a natural power and begins with the observation of nature, then extends to a communication with nature and then to the 'nature of nature' herself. An abstracted, opaque and concrete world is well suited to blocking out this faculty altogether. The rational man of today tends to despise the very supposition of such an energy of perception or may begin to speak of the paranormal. What is normal? Freud was perhaps not far wrong when he described normalcy as neurosis!

Now it seems to me that the Gnostic and the philosopher need each other's contrasting approaches. Sadly, there came in this period a gradual split between them, just as the Gnostic was to be split apart from the Church. I think that this was a tragedy of long-lasting effect. In order to understand how it occurred we need to look at the epoch which both disturbed and inspired both Valentinus and Apuleius. What was wrong with a world which made them so, we may say so desperately interested in finding a point of stability in the strange world of the second century, that period when gnosis emerged in full flower – only to be pruned by the Church Catholic?

Now the moment we begin to hear of a changing, uncertain and perhaps strange world, a little bell may ring in our minds as we think of our time, the late twentieth century. Indeed, there are several important parallels and I think we can learn about our own time by looking at them.

The Second Century – A conversation with Hans Jonas

Professor Hans Jonas has been described as the 'old master' of Gnostic Studies, beginning his studies long before the Nag Hammadi Library had ever been heard of, in the late 1920s in fact – as a student of Martin Heidegger and Rudolph Bultmann in Germany a few years before Hitler came to power. His first major work on the subject appeared in 1934, *Gnosis und spätantiker Geist* (Gnosis and the Spirit of late antiquity) but German scholars risked a great deal if they wanted to review it because the author was a Jew. The influence of the book was thus restricted until after World War II.

Professor Jonas, who, I should add, is emphatically not a gnostic, maintains that the appearance of the Gnostics was a 'world historical event'. He wrote in *The Gnostic Religion* (1958):

> It is the first time in history that the radical ontological [of the nature of essence] difference of man and nature has been discovered and the powerfully moving experience of it given expression in teachings strange and suggestive. This rift between man and nature was never to close again, and protesting his hidden but essential *otherness* became in many variations an abiding theme in the quest for truth concerning man.

In January 1986 at his home in New Rochelle, New York, I discussed with Hans Jonas this point about the significance of the Gnostics in terms of parallels between our time and that of the second century. Professor Jonas began by saying that gnosis:

> is one of the great alternatives in looking at the whole scheme of things and our place in it and, well, do we belong? Or are we aliens? – And if aliens, where do we come from? Where would home be? What would home be? The very fact that they [the Gnostics] probably were the first who saw the theme of the stranger in the world. That makes them, the Gnostics, a world historical event. That theme never disappeared again. It can then re-emerge again and again and if we speak of alienation nowadays, there we are. It has become a perennial theme.

The discussion continued:

AUTHOR: I have been putting forth the thesis that we live in times with remarkable parallels with this period and, let's look at how these particular groups of people dealt with them – do they have anything to teach us? The fear of cosmic catastrophe, apocalyptic expectation, boredom with institutional religion and alienation from the business of running the Empire and being part of that. Would you say that those were the main parallels?

JONAS: Oh yes. Certainly they are the main ones. The climate of rebelliousness is there [in the second century] and leads to very strange intellectual responses and also philosophical responses, as existentialism in our time in this century shows in some of its thinking some parallels with respect to some gnostic thinking and feeling. Certainly there are affinities to the modern situation. We hear these voices from the beginning of the Christian Era. A certain affinity. These things speak to us in a way they wouldn't to, let's say eighteenth-century people. But there is a part that does not strike particular affinities – the whole conception of something otherworldly. We are today very immanentist: everything in the world is – all there is. Their idea that this world is only, that there's something beyond this world which is the true reality and which we find in the tradition of Plato – that is not to do with our thing. So probably the term alienation is a good term to hang up, to hook. There is certainly a widespread unease in the modern mind concerning this age-old question of what is it all about? Are we, are the concerns of the day, the pressing needs of day-to-day existence, is that all there is to it? In perhaps the general disruption in which we live there is a kind of nihilism with which we are confronted – not knowing what the standards are, to what, what way to go in the world, what to expect, what to fear, where to belong, what to guard against and so on. Isn't this the general disorientation? Isn't the feeling that 'everything goes' a sign that something is out of joint? And then we hear these old voices which tell us that the out-of-jointness is not just the accident of a particular situation but somehow belongs to man's being in the world, that we are, though we are part of the world, we are not wholly part of the world, but that our roots may be somewhere else – that we may be exiles. That strikes a chord in us.

AUTHOR: That we're outsiders.

JONAS: Exactly yes. And that we have to chart a way in the world from sources of insight which are not derived from our worldly knowledge alone. Not from what science tells us about causes and effect, or politics or what sociology says about laws of society – the determination theme. That there is a remainder in the equations of our being that is not dissolved into these different forces and determinations. And what is this? This feeling of homelessness points to something. Natural science tells us of an entirely value-free system of forces of which we are a part and this neutrality – value-free, neither hostile nor friendly nor hospitable but it's just plain fact. Brutal fact in which with the forces of our reason and of our inventiveness and so on, we try to carve out as comfortable or acceptable existence for ourselves as we can manage.

AUTHOR: Then a nihilist is a person who has become invaded by the value-free quality of the world?

JONAS: Exactly. The mere indifference of fact, the indifference around us somehow invades ourselves, that nothing ultimately matters and we make things matter for our own purposes.

AUTHOR: What was there in the historical situation of the second-century Empire which might have promoted this feeling? What had been going on in the previous centuries to promote such a feeling of crisis among sensitive people?

JONAS: Well certainly major dislocations of national cultures. From the conquest of Alexander the Great on (334–323 BC), the establishment of cosmopolitan Hellenistic (Greek-influenced) civilization. There the national traditions were somehow driven underground, but in their subterranean survival they then underwent certain changes which, among other things, bred also the spirit of rebelliousness. The official dominant culture which was then taken over in some way by the Roman Empire, especially in its eastern part, did not express the indigenous spirit of the conquered peoples in its new urban civilization.

AUTHOR: Had there been a decline in responsibility to the polis [self governing city]?

JONAS: Very good question, yes. This was a major factor, that, as far as the classical civilization is concerned, it itself had lost its original foundations, namely the life of the polis: the self-governing, autonomous cities. They were now part of an empire in which they had at best become administrative entities but no longer the home for a political self-realization, and this is one factor in the estrangement which people were bound to feel at that time.

AUTHOR: So the individual had become part of a machine?

JONAS: Yes.

One does not have to have read Kafka's *The Trial* or to have seen television's Patrick McGoohan as 'The Prisoner' to find this picture a familiar one. All over the Empire, people were going beyond the received culture in search of a penetrating vision of life which made sense to them. In his *Florida*, Apuleius writes of a certain dissatisfaction with the scope of his education:

> The first cup of knowledge which we receive from our preceptors removes entire ignorance; the second furnishes us with grammatical learning, the third arms us with the eloquence of the rhetorician. Thus far many drink. But I drank of other cups besides these at Athens; of poetry, the fabulous; of geometry, the limpid; of music, the sweet; of dialect, the rough and unpleasant; and of universal philosophy, the never-satiating and nectarious cup.

Ultimately, Apuleius found satisfaction, as many did, by entering into the mystery religion centred about the cult of the Queen of Heaven: Isis. The neophyte, if pure in body and mind, was guaranteed a personal spiritual experience. In Apuleius's moving – and often hilarious – account of his search for spiritual solace, the bestselling *The Golden Ass*, he describes his feelings on beholding a vision of the 'Mother of All':

> ... but my spirit is not able to give thee sufficient praise, my patrimony is unable to satisfy thy sacrifices; my voice hath no power to utter that which I think of thy majesty, no, not if I had a thousand mouths and so many tongues and were able to continue forever.

This kind of initiatory religious experience, especially expressed in a desire to unite with a feminine divine power, was much sought after. It could get quite expensive too. In the melting-pot of the Empire, in which all religions were tolerated – so long as they gave due reverence to the divinity of the Emperor – there was ample opportunity for making acquaintance with oriental cults. Above all, it was the Egyptians who were revered in this age. Egyptian temples were still functioning and devout seekers after religious truth and revelation in the Graeco-Roman world would make pilgrimages to some remotely situated Egyptian temple, passing the night in its vicinity. The hope was that of stimulating dreams in order to receive some vision of divine mysteries. In short, gnosis was on offer in Egypt and many took that offer up as the years passed. They still do. You did not have to go to Bombay. You went to Alexandria. That's where the source was.

I wonder how many parents grieved for lost sons who went off to the great metropolis and then, perhaps, having got the message disappeared off to the desert?

I should say at this point that although the experience of the mystery-religion (whether of Isis, Mithras or Attis) was doubtless akin to that of gnosis, the mystery-religion had a strong natural core involving life-as-a-whole in all its facets. You might feel somewhat alienated before you entered a cult but you came out of it a new man without having lost contact with nature. In the gnosis experience, there is a strong tendency – stronger in some forms than others – to feel apart from nature, to have transcended its laws and obligations. For the Gnostic, broadly speaking, nature was either a swamp or a launching-pad. Or both. In no sense does the essential being the 'pneuma' (spirit) of the Gnostic belong to the earth. He had, as the Nag Hammadi Library's *First Apocalypse of James* puts it: 'not been *caught*'. In short, the world for the Gnostic was a fraud.

Alexandria

Alexandria was a thriving city, a truly cosmopolitan centre for trade – it was the main grain supply for the Imperial armies – for the exchange of ideas, for the development of culture and was in so many respects, the seed-bed for all that was new in the life of the Empire. The old empire of Persia and the remnants of Babylon which had fallen to Alexander the Great, had left many shadows, cultural lines which had never quite disappeared and which began to seep through Alexandria into the West, eroding that sense of the obvious, of the opacity of a confident culture: waves from the past, memories, hopes of release. A curious atmosphere of radical pessimism and an equally radical optimism filled Alexandria's many learning institutions: its museums, its libraries, its schools, its tutors and their pupils. Whatever 'disease' might have been affecting the heart of the Empire, its symptoms would be most surely visible in Alexandria. Perhaps it was akin to the Berlin of the 1980s or more particularly the 1920s. It was somehow apart from the rest of Egypt. The Romans called it Alexandria ad Egyptum – Alexandria-by-Egypt we might say. This sense of separateness no doubt left its thinkers and poets in an ambience of freedom, freedom, that is, to speculate, to invent, to challenge received ideas. When you are at the centre, perhaps the only way to go is upwards – the mind is free to wander. A good deal of the literature coming from Alexandria was concerned with the elevation of the higher mind, the making of wings of the spirit. The concerns of the philosophy schools were timeless. Perhaps, spending a golden spring in Alexandria, the willing pupil could forget about the future with its sense of peril. He could not forget the past. Alexandria was a great centre for the production of books, on history, medicine, natural science, geometry and especially philosophy and religion. For many readers philosophy was religion and religion was philosophy. This conflation could quite often lead to writings which were incomprehensible to non-Alexandrians or were misrepresented by critical readers in say, Rome, where speculation was not so well appreciated. Alexandria was the perfect place for the would-be and real gnostic teacher, philosopher or poet. Even in Rome there would be coteries of the *avant-garde* who would pay for works from Alexandria, doctors from Alexandria, astrologers from Alexandria or religious teachers from Alexandria. From Alexandria came a specialized philosophical theology which would later lead to critical divergencies of thought and expression between the eastern Church centred in Alexandria and Antioch, and the Church in Rome. Even the Bishop of Alexandria, Clement, would write of a Christian gnosis which would make the chief enemy of the Gnostics in the second century, Irenaeus, Bishop of the diocese of Lyon, refer to the gnosis of Valentinus and other gnostic teachers as 'the gnosis falsely so-called'. He was implying thereby that there was a true gnosis. Even this would eventually disappear. Clement in his *Stromateis* (Miscellanies) maintains that gnosis is a special advanced Christianity for the philosophically inclined. In *Book VII* he writes:

> Faith then is a compendious knowledge of the essentials, but gnosis is a sure and firm demonstration of the things received through faith, being itself built up by the Lord's teaching on the foundation of the faith, and carrying us on to unshaken conviction and scientific certainty. As I mentioned before, there seems to me to be a first kind of saving change

from heathenism to faith, a second from faith to gnosis; and this latter, as it passes on into love, begins at once to establish a mutual friendship between that which knows and that which is known. And perhaps he who has arrived at this stage has already *attained equality with the angels*. At any rate, after he has reached the final ascent in the flesh, he still continues to advance, as is fit, and presses on through the holy Hebdomad into the Father's house, to that which is indeed the Lord's abode, being destined there to be, as it were, a light standing and abiding forever, absolutely secure from all vicissitude.

When Clement speaks about 'attaining equality with angels', he is referring to Luke XX. 34–36:

And Jesus said unto them, The sons of this world marry, and are given in marriage: But they that are accounted to attain to that world, and the resurrection from the dead, neither marry, nor are given in marriage: For neither can they die any more: for they are equal unto the angels; and are sons of God, being sons of the resurrection.

In Alexandria then, the Christian and non-Christian was exposed to all manner of influences and lines of thought.

There were Jewish schools, much given to speculation on the nature of God and the constituent beings which constituted his emanation or projection of being. Some of them appear to have been profoundly disappointed with the God of the Old Testament and wrote commentaries on the Jewish scriptures, asserting that the God described there was a lower being, who had tried to blind Man from seeing his true nature and destiny. We hear their echoes in some books of the Nag Hammadi Library, namely, *The Apocryphon of John* and *The Apocalypse of Adam*. They believed in a figure, the 'Eternal Man' or 'Adam Kadmon', who was the glorious reflection of the true God and who had been duped into an involvement with the lower creation, with earthy matter, ruled by an inferior deity who, with his angels made human bodies. They could quote Genesis I. 26: 'Let us make man in our own image.' They believed that the original image of Man, sometimes called Anthrōpos (Greek for Man in the generic sense) had been copied by jealous angels to make the miserable being who was bound to earth. In Ezekiel I. 26 the 'appearance of the likeness of the glory of the Lord' was a 'figure like that of a man'. Man belongs with the divine being – not on earth. The Law, which governed life on earth, was considered to have been the work of a lower deity. These Jewish and Jewish-influenced rebels, so far in thought from their 'countrymen' – though it was probably a long time since their descendants had occupied the same territory – were the intellectual precursors of today's Kabbalists who maintain the tradition that Moses, at Sinai received in addition to the Ten Commandments, a secret understanding of the Divine mind. Some of these people were also Christian to the extent that they believed that the divine figure Jesus had come down to bring back the Gnostic to his true identity within the divine Man, after having robbed the 'Lord of this world' of the hollow victory of the Crucifixion. To some of these rebels, Jesus represented the restoration of the original form of Man: the Glory of God – not His servant. Perhaps some of them were renegades from the Jewish wars of revolt against the Romans, those who may have surrendered the kinds of apocalyptic 'end of the world' hopes that had frequently accompanied these wars. Perhaps they were descendants of the sectaries of Khirbet Qumran who had believed in a final war between the Sons of Light and the Sons of Darkness – but who had internalized this cosmic struggle; in short, they were men who had given up on the world. Some scholars think that gnosis began with these disparate types of Jewish spiritual rebellion and heresy. Not all Gnostics active in Alexandria in this period believed in the necessity of a redeemer figure, whether Jesus or another.

The Hermetists

In the discovery at Nag Hammadi appeared three works which are described as Hermetic. They are *The Discourse on the Eighth and Ninth*, *Asklepios* and the *Prayer of Thanksgiving* from which I quote:

> We give thanks to Thee! Every soul and heart is lifted up to Thee, O undisturbed name, honoured with the name 'God' and praised with the name 'Father', for to everyone and everything (comes) the fatherly kindness and affection and love and any teaching there may be that is sweet and plain, giving us mind, speech, (and) knowledge: mind, so that we may understand Thee, speech, so that we may expound Thee, knowledge, so that we may know Thee. We rejoice, having been illumined by Thy knowledge. We rejoice because thou hast shown us Thyself. We rejoice because while we were in (the) body, Thou hast made us divine through Thy knowledge.

The first thing one notices when one reads this prayer is its evident sincerity, poetry and piety. These are the characteristics of a good deal of Hermetic writing. Why are these writings called Hermetic? They are called so because many of them are written as dialogues between a teacher, Hermes, and his pupils with names such as Tat, Ammon and Asklepios. The names are revealing because they show the syncretistic nature of the discourses, that is, the adaption of Greek and Egyptian thought which inspires them (Asklepios is a Greek name while Tat and Ammon are Egyptian). Some work shows knowledge of Jewish scriptures and this is precisely what we would expect from writings emanating from Alexandria, the city where East and West met. The teachings are guided by one, Hermes Trismegistos, that is, Thrice-Greatest Hermes. The appellation 'Thrice-Greatest' is a dignity of Egyptian origin but Hermes is, of course, a Greek name, properly pronounced as 'Hair-mess' who was the Greek god who, with wings on feet and wings on head (the mind) communicated between earth and heaven. We have heard his melody in Holst's 'Planet Suite' where, as the messenger of the gods, his quick-footed movement is most ably expressed. His is the world of quick-thinking, the flashing insight of the *nous*, the higher reason, and his medium is spirit. This is the condition of mind in which the Hermetic philosopher wishes to operate. It was believed that there was a real man of this name who, according to the Christian poet Lactantius (*circa* AD 400) dwelt in Egypt as a con-temporary or even precedent of Moses. His thought was regarded as having existed earlier than all thinkers, coming from an 'Atlantean' Antiquity. Furthermore, he was held to be the fount from which inspired prophets and philosophers, including Plato, had drunk. He was thought to have been a kind of incarnation of the god Hermes, or the Egyptian equivalent, Thoth – god of writing and magic – and all that stemmed from the quick and inspired wit. Hermes, in short, knew everything there was to know. There are at least 21 books attributed to him and a host of dialogue excerpts. They come from a number of anonymous authors and differ in attitude and often in philosophical content. For example, while some Hermetic writings are written in a pessimistic vein and disparage the world of nature, there is yet a strong and somewhat attractive strain in other Hermetic writings which sees 'God' in every-thing, to the extent that the Hermetic student can enter into that 'mind' of which the universe is an expression:

> The world is the image of God
>
> A great miracle, O Asklepios, is man.

These are two remarkable Hermetic phrases which, as we shall see, were to have a major impact on the first scientific achievements of the Renaissance as well as the philosophy, now called pantheism (God is All and All is God) which to a great extent has informed what we know as romanticism. The home of the Hermetic gnostic is in the projected mind of God.

The Mind in the All is reflected in the *nous* of the subject:

For man is a being of divine nature; he is comparable, not to the other living creatures on earth, but to the gods in heaven, or at any rate he equals them in power. None of the gods in the heaven will ever quit heaven, and pass its boundary, and come down to earth; but man ascends even to heaven, and measures it; and what is more than all beside, he mounts to heaven without quitting the earth; to so vast a distance can he put forth his power. We must not shrink then from saying that a man on earth is a mortal god, and that a god in heaven is an immortal man

(*Libellus* X. 24b–25)

This makes interesting reading in the era of the space shuttle and of the return of magic to the movies. For this is the essence of magic: the transformation of the mind and imagination to enable the subject to work changes in nature in conformity with will. Hans Jonas writes, in a comment on the Hermetic doctrines of the Ascent of the Soul that:

In a later stage of 'gnostic' development (though no longer passing under the name of Gnosticism) the external topology of the ascent through the sphere, with the successive divesting of the soul of its worldly envelopments and the regaining of its original acosmic [that is, not belonging to the cosmos] nature, could be 'internalized' and find its analogue in a psychological technique of inner transformations by which the self, *while still in the body*, might attain the Absolute as an immanent, if temporary, condition: an ascending scale of mental states replaces the stations of the mythical itinerary: the dynamics of progressive spiritual self-transformation, the spatial thrust through the heavenly sphere.

(*Gnostic Religion*, page 165)

The Gnostic believed that at death, his soul would ascend beyond the earth and on, though occasionally obstructed by archons or starry 'governors', to the source of 'Light' within the Pleroma of the Father. In Alexandria, this possibility was seen as one which might be enjoyed before death. The *Discourse on the Eighth and Ninth* in the Nag Hammadi Library describes such an ascent and the wonder of revelation that accompanied it:

For already from them the power, which is light, is coming to us. For I see! I see indescribable depths, How shall I tell you, O, my son? How [shall I describe] the universe? I [am mind and] I see another mind, the one that moves the soul! I see the one that moves me from pure forgetfulness. You give me power! I see myself! I want to speak! Fear restrains me. I have found the beginning of the power that is above all powers, the one that has no beginning. I see a fountain bubbling with life. I have said,

O my son, that I am Mind. I have seen! Language is not able to reveal this. For the entire eighth (sphere), O my son, and the souls that are in it, and the angels, sing a hymn in silence. And I, Mind, understand.

With the Hermetic writings, you got it all!

The body of Hermetic works, the *Corpus Hermeticum*, was written between the second and fourth centuries. They freely interweave congenial Platonist and Stoic philosophy with many concepts circulating in the Alexandria of those centuries. All in all, they make stimulating, inspiring, sometimes dull and occasionally amazing reading for the modern reader unfamiliar with them. At the time they were written, they were intended to be 'teaching-pieces' for small groups – or in one-to-one teaching sessions, and were intended to take the pupil from the position of the disciple 'Tat' or 'Ammon' to the level of insight initiated by the questions and answers of 'Hermes'. If a good pupil, he might come upon an experience of the illuminated mind for the purpose of which the writings were composed. The teacher and pupil would work through the discourses, unveiling layers of meaning in the text to the purpose of unveiling the inner dimensions of the pupil. As the quoted *Prayer of Thanksgiving* implies, it was customary to thank, not Hermes but 'God' for any revelations enjoyed. In all of them, the pupil is 'saved' (from ignorance, from preoccupation with worldly thought and obsession) by the power of his own *nous*. The *nous* was thought to contain the spiritual life-energy which enabled it to ascend the spheres of creation and so behold the incomprehensible *One*. The *nous* was *the* faculty of gnostic perception. We might describe Hermetism as practical or applied philosophy. The Hermetic student was enjoined to avoid contamination with worldly folk: 'And the downward-tending elements of nature were left devoid of reason, so as to be mere matter.' The responsiblity for making matter is sometimes put on the shoulders of 'Mind the Maker'. The first Man was not enmired in such stuff:

> But Mind the Father of all, he who is Life and Light, gave birth to Man, a Being like to Himself. And He took delight in Man, as being His own offspring; for Man was very goodly to look on, bearing the likeness of his Father. With good reason then did God take delight in Man; for it was God's own form that God took delight in. And God delivered over to Man all things that had been made.
>
> (*Libellus* I. 12–13)

At this point, something like a tragedy is said to occur. Man in his ceaseless quest for knowledge breaks through the spheres apportioned to the governors of the lower cosmos (generated by Mind the Maker, a projection of the Father) and proceeds to gaze down to the material waters below. In these he sees his image and, as God delights in Him, He delights in Himself and begins to be attracted downwards. Thus the transmundane (extra-worldly) 'Light' of God becomes trapped in matter.

Now it is highly unlikely that the Hermetic student was meant to take this myth of man's predicament as historical information. It was intended to serve as the text for discussion. For if the attraction in the myth is downwards, it only serves to show that the attraction of the 'Light' in the *nous* works the other way – back to God, back to full consciousness of Man. This whole mood of thought and feeling has doubtless informed the words put into the 'Saviour's' mouth in some of the Nag Hammadi writings. For example in *The Book of Thomas the Contender*, 'Everyone who seeks the truth from true wisdom will make himself wings so as to fly, fleeing the lust that scorches the spirits of men' would not look at all out of place in the Hermetic writings while *The Gospel of Philip*'s 'Saviour' virtually quotes word for word the *Smaragdine Table of Hermes Trismegistus* when he says: 'I came to make [the things below] like the things [above, and the things] outside like those [inside. I came to unite] them in that place.' Hermes might have wished to add: 'So to work the miracle of the one thing.'

There was clearly a good deal of cross-fertilization going on in Alexandria. There were some minds in the Church who regretted this – surely the job of the Church was to bring pagans into the Church and not to convince them that they had enough for salvation already.

But what was Christianity? To a Hermetist, Christ could never be more than a revelation of Mind. This, to a bishop trying to plant the seed of faith in Gaul, for example, was just not enough. The martyrs had not died for this – nor would they die for anything but the Jesus Christ who had died on the Cross 'because God so loved the world that he gave His Only Begotten Son'. 'Mind' does not die on crosses. Of course, for some Gnostics, this was precisely the point. The point was going to get a lot sharper than that before the second century was out. Things were moving within the Church. It was the Gnostics who were indeed going to have to wake up – if they intended staying in the One Church of Christ crucified.

Chapter Three

Madness and Blasphemy

> I do this, in order that thou, obtaining an acquaintance with these things, mayest in turn explain them to all those with whom thou art connected, and exhort them to avoid such an abyss of madness and blasphemy against Christ.

Thus Irenaeus, Bishop of Lyon writes in the Preface to his mammoth literary achievement, *A Refutation and Subversion of Knowledge Falsely So Called* in five volumes. It is usually known simply as *Adversus Haereses – Against Heresies*, and was written in about AD 180. The 'Heresies' are of course 'gnostic' heresies. Of all the works on gnostic 'heresy', this one has been the most influential.

In order to understand how the gnostic movement and its adherents were to become *personae non gratae*, we need to look at Irenaeus and his work. Irenaeus first came to Gaul as presbyter to the missionary Bishop Pothinus. There was a brisk trade between Marseille and Smyrna in Asia Minor and it was Polycarp of Smyrna who instigated the foundation of the See of Lyon. Polycarp was to become one of the most famous martyrs to the Christian cause and stirring accounts of his martyrdom were spread among the churches of East and West. Polycarp had known the Apostle John and it was a harmony of 'Johannine' and 'Pauline' Christianity which held sway in the churches of Asia Minor. Alexandria was on the other side of the world. John had seen the Lord.

So when Pothinus and Irenaeus arrived in Gaul, their position carried the full weight of apostolic authority and commitment. Irenaeus was in a position to put pressure on the Bishop of Rome should it become necessary.

Now in AD 177, the terrible persecution of Marcus Aurelius Caesar was instigated in Lyon, resulting in abiding memories of the 'martyrs of Lyon and Vienne'. Readers are doubtless familiar with the nature of Christian martyrdom in this period – still a popular spectacle for some film producers. During this persecution, Irenaeus was sent to Rome with letters of remonstrance against rising heresy there. The nature of such heresy consisted most visibly in the establishment of extra-church meetings for the *cognoscenti*, the pneumatics, the spiritual aristocracy. These exclusive gatherings were established without authorization of the bishop and, indeed, the Gnostics might well feel that they were outside his jurisidiction as well. The Bishop of Rome himself Eleutherus was patronizing the Montanist heresy which had begun in Phrygia and which held that one, Montanus was the returned Paraclete (Holy Spirit) and that the women, Priscilla and Maximilla, were his prophetesses. Such charismatic fervour is a feature of some churches throughout the world today. The result of such movements for the whole chuch was division and confusion – and this was why all specialist movements had to be brought into line. The only way of accomplishing that was to tighten up the church organization and doctrine centred around the bishop. Since there were prophecies in the New Testament about false prophets and an Antichrist withering away the faithful, it is not surprising that reaction to such movements might become quite hard. In this period, excommunication was the worst that could be done. By the time the Nag Hammadi Library was buried, troublesome (and not troublesome) heretics might suffer death at the hands of an enraged mob or by a local prefect's decision. It would seem that the visit of Irenaeus to Rome marked something of a watershed in his career. Heresy was taking in the missionary's harvest. It should be noted that Rome was a mission of the Greeks, Gaul of Asia Minor while Lyon checks the heretical tendencies of the Bishop of Rome. Rome was not at this point the 'mother and mistress' of the Church.

Returning to Lyon, Irenaeus found Pothinus had died a martyr's death. Irenaeus succeeded him. He was followed it seems by the Valentinians – 'followers' of the now dead Egyptian poet Valentinus who we briefly encountered in the previous chapter. It is likely that Valentinus's followers were rather more loose and adventurous and probably quite outrageous in their reworkings of Valentinus's subtle, imaginative and mythic Christian gnosis.

While in Rome, Irenaeus had also discovered that an old friend from Polycarp's school had also succumbed to a Valentinian-type exposition of the gnosis. This discovery doubtless increased Irenaeus's determination in his life's work. No Christian was to die in the name of vain doctrine, only for the Apostolic Truth as delivered by the Lord to His Apostles and supported by the Jewish scriptures and the four gospels. 'Martyr' means 'witness' and those who had observed and sympathized with the martyrs must know the exact truth to which the deaths bore witness. Valentinians, furthermore, were famous for slipping out of martyrdom by their linguistic subtleties – they shared enough pagan philosophical presuppositions to become indistinguishable from many another eccentric philosophical mystery school. While some Christians even went so far as to see martyrdom as a sacred duty – that is, by imitating Jesus and his demand to 'take up your cross and follow me' – most Gnostics saw no religious value in the destruction of the body. Perhaps some did feel it might assist them on their way, unless, of course, they had not quite achieved a full gnosis, in which case they might have trouble getting past some of the archontic guardians on their way to the Pleroma – so crude had certain gnostic concepts become when in circulation.

Irenaeus, who was himself to die a martyr's death in AD 202, realized that he would have to study the heresies directly. He was confident in the truth for which his brethren had died and there was no need in his mind to exaggerate the doctrines he researched and discussed. His immense and difficult work helped materially to develop and define a catholic doctrine which a century and a half later would without a shadow of doubt exclude the gnosis from the Catholic Church. Up to this time Christian gnosis had been able to develop alongside and within the Christian Church. Irenaeus saw his task as threefold:

1. Render it impossible for anyone to confound the Knowledge with Christianity. (A fairly novel objective – especially in Egypt.)
2. To make it impossible for the gnostic system to survive within the Church.
3. To demonstrate that gnosis (falsely so-called) was of the 'old mythology' and owed its central concepts to pagan philosophy which Christianity came to banish.

It appears he was most successful in this, for after him, there is very little mention of gnostic heresies (certainly as seen as a critical threat) in catholic writing. Then again, Irenaeus had already 'done the business'.

A reading of Irenaeus's work might leave one with the impression that the reasons why gnosis would have to go were principally doctrinal ones, basic disagreements about concepts of God, Christ and the nature of redemption. Professor Elaine Pagels, currently lecturing to theological students at Princeton University, USA, and author of *The Gnostic Gospels*, sees the issue as primarily a political one. She says that it is important to realize that 'every religious tradition except for western Christianity, Islam, Judaism, Buddhism, Hinduism and Greek and

Russian, Coptic and Ethiopic Christianity all had esoteric traditions. Only in the western Christian movement do we see a suppression of that kind of mystical tradition. And I think to find the reason for it – one can look at the time in which it happened. It happened at a time when the Christians were under enormous stress, persecution, potential arrest, public execution; it was important for leaders of Christian groups under that enormous stress to consolidate, to be able to identify who was in the movement and who wasn't. It seems to me that the historical situation, in which public identification, willingness to give one's life in martyrdom, confession of the creeds – identification with that church has a specific political meaning and I think that it was enormously threatening to the leaders of that Church, like Irenaeus, who had suffered terribly under persecution, to see the Church destroyed and fifty or sixty people tortured to death in the Arena of Lyon – an extraordinary thing to live through.'

AUTHOR: And the Gnostics have an ambivalence –

PAGELS: Right, and they say, 'Well, I'm not really!' and suddenly they wouldn't be there. So identifying with the suffering was something Irenaeus felt was essential for the survival of the Church – without that, these groups would simply disappear and be scattered. And so I think it's in that context that the elusive slipperiness of the Gnostics, the willingness to entertain different symbols and different ideas became deeply threatening to the continuity of the Church at that point – and impossible to tolerate. At the same time, historically, Jews were, although 'atheist' from the Roman point of view, they were legal atheists and they could develop a wide range of beliefs including esoteric mystical views. Christians could not tolerate that ambiguity. I think it's because of the kind of stress in which they were living.

There is, I think, another important dimension to consider.

In the previous chapter, we looked at the curious spiritual and political conditions which fostered a feeling of urgency in the second century and which in turn stimulated the attraction of gnosis. Gnosis appeared in times of social, political and religious dislocation, promoting for a minority of the population, an alienation from the world and, for the Gnostic, a withdrawal into *pneuma* (the spirit): the divine aspect of the self was not at home in the world, and neither was it intended to be so. The realization of this gave the gnostic cause for tears and laughter. There was no hope in the world. Now while some Gnostics may not have been so extreme as this, seeing the world as a defective rather than evil product of an inferior being, ignorant of the Incomprehensible Father, and possibly, as the Hermetic writings imply, 'going in' for a degree of pneuma-*projection*-giving value and meaning to an otherwise sadly material world, there is no doubt that most Gnostics believed in an essential antagonism to the material world which was attended to begin with by a good deal of distress and ultimately perhaps a resigned sense of tragedy. Now this feeling was just not the kind of feeling that a catholic Christian could surrender to. The extremity of it is, in this form, simply alien to the kind of atmosphere which prevailed within the Church as Irenaeus knew it. The Church of Irenaeus was a body of hope – hope for the world – and it was precisely the hope expressed in the sufferings of many a martyred Christian that would bring thousands to its cause. When a catholic Christian looked at the world, its sufferings, its capriciousness, its viciousness, he or she knew that it still all made sense. The Christian hope of these people still had a large chunk of apocalyptic consciousness within it. Jesus was expected to return. This was never a gnostic expectation; Christ had ascended – and so must Man. Jesus had worked miracles – bringing nature into accord with the divine will. There are no miracles forthcoming from the gnostic 'Saviour'. Jesus had truly come to earth. He had become, not simply appeared in flesh, as many Gnostics believed. Indeed, he would return to earth and redeem matter while the faithful Christian could expect to be resurrected in the body, no longer subject to corruption. For the Gnostic, the body was a disposable 'tunic', prison or tomb. The dynamics of salvation lay not in the determination of the Gnostic but within an historical event prefigured by the resurrection of Christ and controlled by Him. In short, Irenaeus and the Gnostics were aeons apart and the split between them would surely have come whether the Church of Irenaeus had been persecuted or not. Gnosis as it was developed in the time of Irenaeus could never be 'esoteric Christianity' – a concept wholly alien to the mainstream of catholic and orthodox Christianity.

There is a strong possibility that the Gnostic was consciously in opposition to the apocalyptic hope, which is, as Irenaeus expresses it, at the very end of his *Against Heresies*:

> the resurrection of the just, and the inheritance in the kingdom of the earth; and what the prophets have prophesied concerning it harmonize....
> The apostle [Paul] too, has confessed that the creation shall be free from the bondage of corruption, into the liberty of the sons of God....
> Subsequently bestowing in a paternal manner those things which neither the eye has seen, nor the ear has heard, nor has [thought concerning them] arisen within the heart of man.

The last sentence here, a quotation from I Corinthians II. 9 is most instructive. Firstly, the words are apparently put into the mouth of the

Living Jesus of *The Gospel of Thomas*: 'I shall give you what no eye has seen and what no ear has heard and what no hand has touched and what has never occurred to the human mind.' There are some subtle changes – for 'mind' read 'heart' – in the Pauline version.

Secondly, the chapter of I Corinthians, from which it is taken, describes how the Church in Corinth – not an esoteric church – has come to know the meaning of the presence of Christ in the world: 'But unto us God revealed them through the Spirit: for the Spirit searcheth all things, yea, the deep things of God' (*verse* 10). Paul rounds off his description of the blessedness of the spiritual gift by saying: 'For who hath known the mind of the Lord, that he should instruct him? But we have the mind of Christ' (*verse* 16).

Where Irenaeus sees such revelations as coming to the faithful Christian after the 'resurrection of the just', Paul himself speaks of them as the shared experience of the Corinthian Church. The Gnostics saw them as the province of an élite. Between the two most extreme poles, only Paul perhaps could have found a reconciliation. Both the Catholic and the Gnostic were perhaps now two extreme conditions of a once more temperate climate. Then again, as Blake begs us to consider, does not the 'Road of Excess' lead 'to the palace of wisdom'. In the political world, a reckoning was inevitable.

What was wrong with the Gnostics?

We have seen that the Gnostic did not really share in the 'ambience' of main stream catholic Christianity – particularly in the western churches. Now being somewhat alien from the world, if not from the unknown God of the gnostic heart, the individual Gnostic would be more likely to feel the necessity of finding answers to those ultimate questions that many of us, as we grow older, prefer to leave unanswered as we are more and more drawn into the necessities of day-to-day living. If you ask a nun, for example, working in a refugee camp, 'Where does evil come from?', she might ask you to look around for a while and then say that she hasn't the time – she's too busy dealing with its effects. In our demanding world it is attractive to say simply, 'I don't know.' A-gnosis makes for a kind of pragmatic clarity: 'We're living in a material world. And I am a material girl!' took the pop star Madonna to the top of the charts. Many a student leaves philosophy behind when he or she heads for the top of his or her profession. The Gnostic, less involved, and with a desire to extricate himself from the bindings of the world, had a positive yearning for experiential knowledge. The second-

The Jabal al-Tarīf in the vicinity of Hamra Dūm where the 'Nag Hammadi' Library was discovered in December 1945. The library was found near a large boulder which had fallen to the foot of the cliff, approximately at the centre of this photograph.

Images of images: thirty-four years after the discovery, Muḥammad Alī sees himself in a copy of *Biblical Archaeologist*, Fall 1979, as revealed to him by Valerie Kaye.

Professor Gilles Quispel is reunited with the *Jung Codex* at the Coptic Museum, Cairo, in 1986.

Where seekers came to dream – in the 2nd century. Now dreamers come to seek. An Egyptian temple is the proper setting for the Hermetic student. This temple in Luxor was an ancient monument even in late antiquity. The stone images were thought to have absorbed the divine wisdom called down by centuries of belief and magical practice.

Forty years after the discovery Gilles Quispel meets Muḥammad Alī al-Sammān: 'Well I'm so very pleased to meet you.'

The Coptic Museum in old Cairo where the Nag Hammadi Library now rests beneath plexi-glass.

Professor Gilles Quispel is reunited with Dr Pahor Labib, former director of the Coptic Museum and the first man to prepare a photographic edition of *The Gospel of Thomas*.

No time for Christians. A Roman officer and his wife from 2nd-century Nîmes. This particular officer was a devotee of Mithras, the conquering deity of the sun, beloved among soldiers.

A Christian sarcophagus from 3rd-century Arles. Old Testament and New Testament stories are seen as a continuum. Gnostics disapproved of this orthodox vision. Right of top centre, one can see Moses receiving the law. For Gnostics this act represented a submission of Humanity to a deficient god: the Demiorgos.

Bishop Irenaeus (Raymond Ross) takes a patronising view of the Gnostic (Paul Dixie) believing him to be dwelling in 'an abyss of madness and blasphemy.' Was he right?

A Cross from Les Cassès in Languedoc. Its form is apparently akin to a Bogomil image discovered in Bulgaria. The Christ appears triumphant *on* the Cross and it seems to this author that the sculptor is more inspired by a heterodox sense of the spirit of Humanity than by the orthodox image of a suffering Jesus, forsaken and bleeding.

The fortified town of Minerve where 140 Cathar *perfecti* were burned in a single summer's day in 1210.

The historian R.I. Moore in the market-place of Fanjeaux.

The Cathar Guilhabert de Castres (Brian Blessed) faces the Pope's envoy, Dominic Guzman (Ian Brooker). The confrontation ended in impasse. 'When a blessing fails, a good thick stick may succeed,' Dominic is reported to have said. What kind of 'success'?

century Latin apologist (for Christianity), Tertullian, wrote that, 'the questions that make people heretics are. Where does humanity come from and how? Where does evil come from and why?' This was a typical no-nonsense, no-gnosis approach from the mind of a Latin legalist who would later join the Montanists (enthusiast-charismatics). The moment we talk of experiential knowledge, we are coming closer to the kind of approach that so baffled and enraged such men as Irenaeus. For the gnosis was thought to be best expressed in the manner of imaginative myths – in a similar manner to the understanding that many people have gained from watching the fictional episodes of TV's 'Star Trek' or in the realm of the science-fiction novel. Whether we like it or not, this was the way that many Gnostics came to understand their predicament. There were many variations in these gnostic accounts of how the world came to be fatally flawed and of how the Gnostic came to feel a stranger in the world. Indeed, Irenaeus complains that the Gnostics make it their business to invent some new opinion every day. For the Gnostic, who felt himself to be dealing with the unknown this was quite permissible – the system had to fit in the experience (a very different attitude from philosophy in general) and anyway, it was a sign of the Gnostics having the gift of creative insight: the hallmark of being a gnostic was to be an 'original'.

In the gnostic 'systems' that Irenaeus analysed, there was a paradox from the start. They were systems to explain the unfathomable. Although philosophical or scientific knowledge was not expected to proceed from the system, an inner sense of knowing was.

The Valentinian System

Irenaeus devotes a lot of time to undermining this system. It is quite complicated and I hope I shall be forgiven for simplifying it. Before doing so, it might be helpful to know something of the man who is thought to have conceived it.

Valentinus was born in about AD 110 in Egypt. There he distinguished himself as a poet and a man of considerable talents in the field of philosophical theology. He was an eloquent man of great personal magnetism and his reputation was such that as late as the beginning of the fifth century St Jerome would say of him: 'No one can bring an influential heresy into being unless he is possessed by nature of an outstanding intellect and has gifts provided by God. Such a man was Valentinus.' He was apparently a visionary, saying that when young he had a dream of the Logos (briefly, the energy which created the universe) appearing to him in the form of a child. This man took his dreams seriously and perhaps today we are better placed to recognize the value of dreams than say, Irenaeus was. Valentinus was in Rome in the middle of the second century and nearly became bishop – which must say something about the nature of the Church in Rome at that time. His opponents said that it was failure to become a bishop that led to his secession from the Church.

The Valentinian system begins like this: let us say that at the very Beginning there was already an eternity of being, a Pleroma, a Fullness, a Harmony. At the 'centre' was always the Father, perfect and immeasurably profound – a being of whom nothing could be said which would share in the character of the eternity of which he was. Now it is of the nature of the Father to project a series of archetypes. They are Intelligence (Nous), Truth, the Word (Logos), Life, Humanity and Church (an invisible, eternal body). These archetypes hold a potential energy and they in turn project a series of archetypes. With each projection, the archetype finds itself to be at a 'distance' from the Father – but there is no real distance for there is no space and time. All this is happening in a dimension so removed from the one we know that there is no real way of describing it. The whole thing is an intuition – the activity of the *nous* within the Gnostic's own experience – philosophical poetry.

Now it is of the nature of wisdom, when active, to question and strive to understand. One of the projections, Sophia (Wisdom) begins to be unbalanced within the Pleroma because 'she' wishes to know the Father – a privilege granted only to Nous who is closer to the Father. The archetypes contain, as I said, a potential which though the Father is ultimately responsible for, he does not choose to control. The disturbance within Sophia leads to her conceiving 'substance without form'. It has come from guilty yearning and so is flawed. It is of a lesser substance. The Pleroma is shaken but the 'Limit' of the Pleroma convinces Sophia that the Father is incomprehensible. The product of her passion is discarded from the Pleroma into the All, a void. The Father sees a necessity to project two more archetypes: Christ and the Holy Spirit who teach the contents of the Pleroma their true relation to the Father. The Pleroma sings the praises of the Father and the 'perfect fruit' of their joy comes into being: the saviour Jesus. All is not well, however. 'Substance without form', exiled from the Pleroma brings matter to birth out of her anguish and yearning for Christ as well as a psychic or 'soul' element. 'Christ' has pity for her and descends to put form on her formlessness which in turn brings about *pneuma*: spirit. Out of these three elements: soul, matter and spirit the 'world' is created.

So solid things owe their source to 'broken' Ideas.

Sophia forms a 'demiurge' – a creator – to make something out of the mess that has come about. He organizes heaven, earth and the creatures which live on it. Most importantly, we can see that this 'demiurge' is a rather poor copy of the eternal archetypes, and is identified with the God of the Old Testament – a deficient being who seems unaware of his deficiency and is determined that his creatures shall remain unaware of their source. Three types of men are said to exist: carnal types (material beings who have no chance of saving gnosis), psychic types (who can achieve a salvation by the knowledge and imitation of Christ) and of course, pneumatic types, who since they have the divine *pneuma* within them only have to make the connection between their *pneuma* and 'Jesus' and they are saved. The pneumatic on awakening can make a swift return to the Pleroma. Furthermore, the pneumatic-gnostic is superior to the demiurge.

Needless to say, Irenaeus, when encountering this myth, was horrified. He proceeded in *Against Heresies* to tear it to pieces. The basis on which he did so was to have momentous effects for the history of Christianity. The one key question that Irenaeus asks is: where did all this come from? The system follows neither scripture nor apostolic tradition. There is a perpetual succession of bishops from the apostles and none of them has ever taught like this. Thus, the position of the bishop, his authority in matters of doctrine was strengthened. He says the Valentinians 'maintain that they have attained to a height beyond every power, and that therefore they are free in every respect to act as they please, having no one to fear in anything. For they claim that because of the *redemption* ... they cannot be apprehended, or even perceived by the judge.' As Professor Pagels puts it: 'Gnosis offers nothing less than a theological justification for refusing to obey the bishops and priests!' Irenaeus obviously did not like the Gnostics he came across. They seemed somewhat 'unchristian' in their attitudes and rather unnatural as well: 'If anyone yields himself to them like a little sheep, and follows out their practice and their *redemption*, such a person becomes so puffed up that ... he walks with a strutting gait and a supercilious countenance, possessing the pompous air of a cock!'

The 'redemption' appears to have been a gnostic initiation rite, 'freeing' the Gnostic from the grip of the demiurge and his 'hit-beings', the archons. 'What price freedom?' Irenaeus asks. As for the 'cock', gnostic charms and statuettes have been found featuring the body of a man and the head of a cock, laughing at, presumably, the world and its cares. The figures are sometimes called 'Abraxas', a 'being of light' in which opposites of 'good' and 'evil' are transcended in the morally neutral realm of Spirit. The symbol of the cock presumably derives from the observation that the cock is the first animal to greet the morn. Some Gnostics liked to think of themselves this way, as an *avant garde* of the human race. Today, we still call some people 'cocky' and some misinformed writers today translate gnostic as 'know-all' and apply the type to Marxist 'philosophers' who claim a superior insight into the workings of the world and its 'true' destiny.

Irenaeus asserts that the Truth is only to be found in the Catholic Church 'for prior to Valentinus, those who follow Valentinus had no existence' – that is to say that Valentinus has no authority to talk of Christ because his teachings are original. Valentinus himself is thought to have claimed that he obtained his higher gnosis from Theodas, a pupil of Paul. Irenaeus explicitly asserts that the Gnostics 'possess more gospels than there really are' but his reasons for holding to the key number of four are perhaps less than convincing today. There are four zones of the world, there are four winds, the Cherubim of Psalm LXXX have four faces, there were four covenants with God; 'the pillar and ground of the Church is the Gospel and the spirit of *life*'. It is, therefore, fitting that there are four pillars 'vivifying man afresh'. Irenaeus goes through a whole host of accusations based, it must be stressed, on the Valentinian 'creation myth'. He says that Divine wisdom cannot have 'guilty yearnings' – how could Divine wisdom go wrong? He also says that souls continue to exist in the body-form which is therefore not a prison; that 'no man hath seen God at any time' (John I. 18) – only the Son can declare what is invisible and so Valentinus cannot therefore speak of the content of the Godhead (the Pleroma). Above all, the most damning belief that the Gnostics share is that the Father of Jesus is not the same being as the creator of the heavens and the earth. This was a deadly serious matter. The belief in a demiurge, a great architect of the universe as being distinguishable from the incomprehensible 'God' in his essential being was not an invention of the Gnostics. Plato speculated on the existence of the demiurge and some concept of 'him' was widespread in the philosophy schools at the time. What was so terribly disturbing, what, in fact, put the sting into gnosis was the notion of an opposition between the eternal Father and the architect. This would cause sparks in the philosophy schools of the Neoplatonists which were developing in Alexandria and which cared nothing for Christianity. So Irenaeus could, if he wanted, find a rational concensus in the intellectual world around him which would be equally horrified at the stress on the perversity and inferiority of the creator.

But what did Gnostics really think about the demiurge?

If for a moment we imagine an impossible image. Across the expanse of space flies a being of tremendous size, nine times the size of this planet. He hovers about earth, darkening the skies and proceeds to implant an image of his face in the minds of the entire population of earth who are, naturally, thunderstruck. Then he speaks so all can understand him. He says, 'For a long time you have heard of me. For a long time you have waited for me. Here I am. I have decided to take away the pain of childbirth from women; I have planted trees in your gardens and parks whose fruit will be gold and silver. There will be so much that no one can ever have more than another. Poverty will vanish. I have removed all dangerous bacteria and everyone will live to a hundred without ever knowing pain. All I ask is that you do as I say...' The Gnostic turns away and says, 'Not likely!' He turns to the crowds and says, 'I bet you think this is God. Come on, surely, the thought has crossed your mind. You're not sure, some of you, and those that are not sure, come with me a while.' A little later, those who had gone with the Gnostic return to the city and, dodging all those who are busily collecting their gold and silver and rushing to their banks – just in case – stand in a line and shout together, 'Hey you up there!' The being looks down at them. And they all put their tongues out. At that moment, the being disappears and the Gnostics have to run very fast to escape all those who hate them. This is pretty much how a gnostic might see the demiurge. The demiurge is an image, an image of 'God' which we have conjured in our minds, or an image which exists in the being of this tragic creation – a part of the fabric of suffering that goes with it.

The Valentinian Gnostics in particular were very suspicious of words, even their own. Elaine Pagels has studied the way that these Gnostics thought about religious language. They seem to have thought that words could become part of the 'bindings', part of the great irreality which produces intoxication in us, drunkenness or sleep. The Gnostic has to break through this dullness of sense, to look through this whole fraud of the world, this Deception which struts around in so many forms and under so many names:

The Valentinian Gnostics, like others, pointed out that most Jews and Christians think of God the creator in certain ways. They think of God as creator, father, judge, lord. They had these pictures in their minds of Him. They expressed a lot of interest in the way that we use words to talk about reality. And that when we use words – I'm thinking of *The Gospel of Philip* – that says that when we use the word 'God' or 'resurrection' or 'Jesus' or whatever, we're not talking about the realities that those words express, but we're talking about our mental image of whatever those realities conjure up. And I think that is an effort to remind us that all of language is a purely symbolic system, especially religious language, and that it only comes to life when there's some kind of inner experience that transforms us from which our language emerges. And they also wanted to point out that the story of creation as they saw it was not to be taken literally. That they believed all things had come from a divine source that was much deeper and stranger than the picture of the creator as the book of Genesis portrays him.

(*Elaine Pagels, 1986*)

If this is the case, then Irenaeus has taken the Valentinian myth much too literally. Valentinus thought mythologically. Irenaeus did not. This whole spiritualized vision of reality is foreign to Irenaeus and the bulk of the apostolic tradition – certainly as he understood it.

Now this all sounds as if the Gnostics were subtle thinkers to a man and woman, but this is most unlikely. For many Gnostics, this experience of gnosis was essentially a simple and intuitive one. In the National Museum of Rome, there exists an inscription to the memory of one Flavia Sophē. It is about 15 inches high and comes from Rome in the third century. It is a very touching memorial of a man to his deceased wife. It is all that remains inscribed in stone testifying to the gnostic presence in Rome. It reads:

> Longing for the light of the Father, my relation and companion of my bed Sophie, anointed in the bath of Christ, with imperishable unction, you went to see the faces of the aeons, the angel of the Great Council, the true Son.

Professor Gilles Quispel has said that it should be seen as 'a symbol of the love of Christ and His Church that didn't see marriage for the progeny of children, but that there's something religious in sexual intercourse itself, longing for God. . .'. Since the Holy Spirit was regarded as feminine, sex for those Gnostics who were not ascetics, could have a sacramental aspect. This understanding was confused by orthodox writers with those gnostic extremists who held that those who had been freed from the 'god of the Law' were free to behave how they chose and among whom the cultic orgy was practised. Namely the followers of the gnostic teacher Carpocrates who coined the proto-communist dictum: 'Property is theft'. The idea was that by consciously sinning one would thereby uncoil oneself from the grip of the unconscious power of sin; a corollary of the gnostic demand, 'know thyself'. Consequently, the Gnostics in general, were long regarded as infamous sexual deviants and moral libertines. Today too, groups in Europe and America dignify their 'love-cults' with the name 'gnostic'. Whenever there is a deviation from the societal norm there appears to be a mechanism within the detractors' minds which immediately conjures up images of sexual perversion – especially when those movements are particularly favourable to women, as the Valentinian gnosis certainly was, and which give women places of authority or equality. As Kurt Rudolph writes in *Gnosis*:

> The percentage of women was evidently very high and reveals that gnosis held out prospects otherwise barred to them, especially in the official Church. They frequently occupied leading positions either as teachers, prophetesses, missionaries or played a leading role in cultic ceremonies (baptism, eucharist) and magical practices (exorcisms).

Quispel has said that gnosis gave women the right to, and experience of, the Self.

In the 'Berlin Codex' (4th–5th centuries), there exists a fragment of *The Gospel of Mary* in which Mary Magdalene rebukes Peter (and by extension the exclusively male bishops) for being too dominant and says that Jesus held her in a special esteem, granting her a gnosis of the divine world. In *The Gospel of Philip*, there is the record of how Jesus used to kiss Mary on the mouth, provoking the disciples to ask why Jesus loves her more than them, to which he cryptically replies, 'Why do I not love you like her?' and proceeds to relate an allegory to the effect that Mary has seen the 'Light' while others remain blind. It should be remembered that Mary was the first to witness the Resurrection and it seems that Gnostics took the trouble to consider what this might have meant. Of course, today we tend to think of women as having a better developed intuitive faculty and many a man has been indebted to a woman's wisdom. The Valentinian Gnostics certainly seem to have had a more balanced view of the sexes than that which many of us have inherited. They said that intercourse is good for your spiritual development. 'It's completely unique in the whole history of Christianity and Judaism. And that was founded in that idea of polarity (male and female forming a whole, equally) which is essential for gnosticism,' says Gilles Quispel. Other texts, however, speak of androgyny as the nature of the perfect or original Man while others tend to think that females should become males but that this male identity lies within themselves – and likewise, that men have also an inner feminine identity. These particularly are strands of thought which were taken up with alacrity by medieval and Renaissance alchemists who were also fascinated by the many unexplored aspects of the human-being, and of whom Jung has written so convincingly in his book *Psychology and Alchemy* (1943).

Lastly, Irenaeus writes with particular distaste of the association of gnostic ideas with magical practice. The essence of such activity has been dealt with in the section on the Hermetists. It is quite obvious that Irenaeus does not really know much about this. Nevertheless, he continues the almost certainly erroneous tradition that the Gnosis began with magicians; in particular, with Simon Magus, a figure who appears in the canonical Acts of the Apostles as one who tried to buy the spiritual power of the apostles and whose vain efforts have given us the word 'simony' to describe those who try to buy their way to power – now very much an approved past-time. The point being here that the spirit of the Gnostic was essentially a counterfeit one – a plastic spirit.

It was an amazing experience to find, in the Bibliotheca Philosophica Hermetica in Amsterdam, recently how this tradition had reached the German scholar-magician Henry Cornelius Agrippa (1486–1535), author of the widely influential (in his day) *Three Books of Occult Philosophy*. In his *Of the Vanitie and Uncertaintie of Artes and Sciences* (English translation 1569), Agrippa writes in the 48th chapter:

> Of the Magitiens also is sprung in the Church a great route of heretickes, which as Iamnes and Mambres have rebelled against Moses, so they have resisted the Apostolicke truth: the chief of these was Simon the Samaritaine, who for this Arte had an image erected at Rome in the time of Claudius Caesar with this inscription, to Simon the holy GOD. His blasphemies be written at large by Clement, Eusebius and Irenaeus. Out of this Simon as out of a seed plot of all heresies, have proceeded by many successions the monstrous Ophites, the filthy Gnostickes, the wicked Valentinians, the Cerdonians, the Marcionites, the Montanians, and many other hereticks, for gain and vaine glory speaking lies against God, availing nor profiting men, but deceiving and bringing them to ruin and destruction, and they which believe in them shall be confounded in God's judgement.

Agrippa had read, with approval and as an authority, the Hermetic writings. I wonder what he would have made of the Nag Hammadi Library? Would he have found the 'filthy gnostickes' there?

Irenaeus rested his case.

The End of the first great Gnostic Movement

We do not really know how it was that a movement which had clearly been seen as a threat by Irenaeus and which appears to have been in every sense a challenge to incipient catholicism came to virtually disappear from the history of the Christian Church. It is certain that after the transmission of Irenaeus's work and the work of other authorities in the Church, individual churches had much stronger grounds for expelling the unrepentant Gnostic from the congregation. They also had the approval of the bishops and the principle was firmly established: 'when in doubt, refer to the bishop'. It is presumed that bishops may have welcomed this. Gnosis has been described as 'the shadow of the Church' and it is likely that when it no longer operated within an existing system, it did not have the capacity to produce an alternative long-lasting structure. Principally, this must have been because it was not ideologically suited to making an institution with the power of longevity. Gnostics were not very interested in the argument: 'we have been here for two or three hundred years, therefore we have solid and attestable foundations'. They did not require the sealed approval that we find on many products today – 'By Appointment'. . . . For this reason, it is likely that Gnosis, as a movement, was self-defeating. Furthermore, its appeal to the 'elect' who by definition must be few, would see it whittle down to a virtual 'club-membership'. Again, it must be stressed that the Gnostics were not interested in 'seeing it all out' until Jesus returned with angels and trumpets sounding. When you had received the 'Light', you were effectively out of history. We should, therefore, not condemn the Gnostics because they did not have the equivalent of an English Constitution guaranteed to absorb dissent and centralize itself about unimpeachable authority – 'the people'. Indeed, from a gnostic point of view, the 'success' of the Catholic Church really only demonstrated its failure to hold to a truly spiritual message – going for outwardly durable foundations at the expense of inner growth.

We know from the burial and discovery of the Nag Hammadi Library that small coteries continued to espouse the Christian and non-Christian gnosis but were more and more 'driven to the hills' or, rather, the sands of the desert. This place was perhaps especially suitable for them as they reflected upon what a desert existed within the mind of the 'world'.

In David Lean's *Lawrence of Arabia*, when Lawrence is asked by a Chicago reporter as to why he likes the desert, Lawrence looks him up and down and says, 'Because it's *clean*.' Appearing and disappearing in and through history would prove to be the Gnostic's only way of staying free.

I asked the 'old master' of Gnostic studies, Hans Jonas, what the Church might have lost by excluding the Gnostics. He replied, 'Well perhaps a spirit of daring, individual daring, and thinking about the mysteries of being and the godhead. Every orthodoxy somehow becomes rigid, but this is probably one of the conditions of its being long-lived. Their inventiveness could not be tolerated. There would not have been a consolidated church with its dogma if that would go on, and the suppression of it meant of course a loss. A loss of a vividness which however from time to time rose again in the Church itself, in the heretical movements of the Middle Ages.'

Before we move on in time and space some 800 years to look at those heretical movements of the Middle Ages, and in particular the Cathars, there are perhaps two other factors we should consider.

Firstly, many Gnostics may have become absorbed in the attempt of the prophet Mani's construction of a universal religion on Gnostic and dualist lines. By dualist I mean the thought which sees all reality for man as being a conflict between opposing principles of 'Light' and 'Darkness', Spirit and Matter. Mani, who came from the region of Baghdad in modern-day Iraq had his first vision in about AD 240 where he saw himself as 'Apostle of Light'. The religion he founded, which contained Zoroastrian, Christian, Jewish, Buddhist and Gnostic thought was to become enormously successful, to the extent that under Theodosius I, being a Manichee carried the death penalty (375–395). St Augustine became a Manichee between 373–382 but later turned against them. It was perhaps his Manichee experience that enabled Augustine to describe mankind as a 'lump of sin' but this is disputed. Some would argue that main-stream Christianity could easily have furnished him with such thoughts. Manicheism resisted persecution and by the ninth century Central Asia was Manichean. In 719 there was a Manichean church in Peking and the Manichees were strong in central and western Asia until the thirteenth century when it would appear that they were wiped out during the Mongol conquests. Mani, who called himself, the 'seal of the prophets' would, of course, lose the dignity to the founder of Islam.

Secondly, there was a great movement in the third and fourth centuries away from paganism and toward Christianity and the Gnostics seem to have suffered in this movement too. The easy way between being a pagan and a Christian enjoyed (by some) in the second century seemed to have vanished. A hardening in the arteries of the Empire seems to have taken place and this culminated in the fourth century with the closure of many pagan institutions and places of worship. Egypt seems to have suffered particularly in this 'wind of change' and it is perhaps from this period that some lone voice composed the lament for vanished times which appears in the Nag Hammadi version of the Hermetic dialogue *Asklepios* and which was to return in the late fifteenth century as a herald for a new current in what has been described as the rebirth the Renaissance.

> And Egypt will be made a desert by the gods and the Egyptians. And as for you, O River, there will be a day when you will flow with blood more than water. And dead bodies will be (stacked) higher than the dams. And he who is dead will not be mourned as much as he who is alive. Indeed the latter will be known as an Egyptian on account of his language in the second period (of time). O Asklepios, why are you weeping? He will seem like (a) foreigner in regard to his customs. Divine Egypt will suffer evils greater than these. Egypt, lover of God, and the dwelling place of the gods, school of religion, will become an example of impiousness.

> And in that day the world will not be marvelled at.... It has become neither a single thing nor a vision. But it is in danger of becoming a burden to all men. Therefore, it will be despised – the beautiful world of God, the incomparable work, the energy which possesses goodness, the many-formed vision, the abundance that does not envy, that is full of every vision. Darkness will be preferred to light and death will be preferred to life. No one will gaze into heaven. And the pious man will be counted as insane, and the impious man will be honoured as wise. The man who is afraid will be considered as strong. And the good man will be punished like a criminal.

PART TWO

The Good Men

Chapter Four

The Good Men

And the good man will be punished like a criminal
(From Hermetic Dialogue between
Hermes Trismegistos and Asklepios.
circa 3rd century)

Introduction

An awful lot of rubbish has been written about the subject of Catharism. The Cathars have been seen as mysterious transmitters of an esoteric doctrine with powerful magical and mystical implications. They have been seen as being in some way connected to the myths surrounding the Holy Grail, King Arthur, primordial and pagan 'gnosis' and quite recently have been tied to one of the most florid of modern conspiracy theories involving everything from Christ's alleged descendants, the Merovingian dynasty, the Knights Templar, the House of Lorraine, nineteenth- and twentieth-century theosophy and occultism, the Nazi Party, Rosicrucianism, Symbolist poetry, the painter Nicolas Poussin, the Ark of the Covenant to the now familiar mélange of inter-galactic UFOlogy, 'Holism', cosmogonic speculation, Ancient Egyptian Mythology, quests for Atlantis and prehistoric astronomy. These strains of anti-rational and quasi-religious investigations are part of the weakness of our times. They are witnesses to an alienation from a scientific movement which seems to leave Man helpless among physical determinations which make us feel that we are unnecessary. It is a pity that the historical Cathars have, as it were, got mixed up in all of this. Deceased members of our species have, of course, no 'will' in the matter of how later generations will use them. It is sometimes left to the laborious business of historians to quietly keep as true as possible a record of what really happened. Not all historians have 'clean hands' in this process but we have been fortunate that post-war historians, palaeographers and archivists have exercised their duties with considerable thought and care. Part Two of this book 'The Good Men' owes its substance to their work – a work, it should be added, that is still in progress and therefore future readers may well be in a position to disagree with the formulations and understandings which constitute the following description.

The Sources

The facts about Catharism are considerably more interesting than the myths. What are those facts based on? In the year 1163 an assembly of Catholic bishops took place in Tours, the administrative centre for the Loire Valley in northwestern France. The assembly decided that stern measures should be taken against a new heresy that had appeared in Gascony and Provence and which was spreading like a cancer. That is the first certain reference to the arrival in France of the Cathar 'heresy' which had appeared in Cologne, Bonn and Liège some twenty years earlier. The heresy was also to be called 'Manichean'. These 'heretics' were not Manichean. They never refer to Mani, the prophet of the Manichees and although they shared certain characteristics of Manicheism, the heretics themselves thought of themselves not as representatives of a new revelation, as the Manichees did, but as true or good Christians. Their chief source of doctrine was the New Testament, holding particular attention to *The Gospel of John* and the other three gospels. The word 'Cathar' comes from the Greek word καθαρος (katharos) meaning 'unpolluted' and although this was not a word which they applied to themselves with great readiness, it is still not as abusive a term as 'Manichean' had become and it does tell us something about their attitude to Christianity – they were devoted to the pure spiritual light whose true home is with the Good God in heaven.

During the years that followed the assembly at Tours, the Cathars rapidly gained supporters and sympathizers in very well defined areas. There were no Cathars to be found in Languedoc to the east of the Rhone valley and very few west of the Garonne. They were to be found in the counties of Toulouse, Albi, Carcassonne, Béziers and the county of Foix. There are good reasons for this as we shall see. The Cathars were to play a central role in a series of dramatic and, indeed, traumatic events which formed one of the turning-points in the history of the kingdom of France and of western Europe. Those events and the Cathar beliefs are extremely well documented. There is a large amount of chronicle evidence. There is vernacular poetry which includes the epic *Le Chanson de la Croisade* largely written by the troubadour Guillaume de Tudèle. The Chanson (Song) describes the Crusade mounted against the 'Albigenses' as the Cathars were often called by their enemies. ('Albigenses' because an enclave of heretics had early on been exposed in Albi). Above all there are the records of the Inquisition. The Inquisitors were active in the Languedoc by order of the Pope so as to secure confessions and, sometimes, to discover the nature of the heresy itself. Thousands of these interrogations still survive in the archives of the Bibliothèque Nationale in Paris, in the Vatican Library and in the city archives of Carcassonne and Toulouse. These reveal not only a great deal about the beliefs of the Cathars but also, as Emmanuel Le Roy Ladurie's book *Montaillou* has demonstrated, about the details of their way of life.

In a similar manner to that by which our knowledge of the first Gnostics was much improved by the Nag Hammadi discovery, our knowledge of Catharism has greatly benefitted from discoveries made in the twentieth century. A short time before World War II, Father Dondaine discovered the *Liber de duobus Principiis* (Book of the Two Principles) in Florence. An anonymous treatise contained in the *Liber contra Manicheos* was found in two versions in Prague and in Paris. This material along with the works *Les Questions de Jean* (The Questions of John) which describes St John in heaven asking questions of Christ as to the origin of the world (which is held to be a tragedy), a Cathar prayer incorporated in the inquisition records of the Bishop of Pamiers, Jacques Fournier, and a Cathar Church 'Ritual' (in Latin and Occitan – the *langue* [language] *d'oc* which gave this region its name) are all from the thirteenth century when many Cathars, it seems, fled to their spiritual brethren in the region of Concorezzo in Italy. These works were composed by the *bons hommes* (good men) themselves.

The Arrival of the Cathars in twelfth-century Languedoc – The Buggers

The exact origins of the Cathars are quite obscure. Nevertheless, there is a pattern of movement that can be discerned from the time of the ninth century in Armenia. It was in the marginal and mountainous regions of those parts that Gnostics and other heretics of various persuasions had taken refuge from those edicts of the emperors of Constantinople which had made heresy a capital crime. Among these outlaws were the so-called Paulicians, a sometimes warlike sect of an apparently mixed 'Manichean'-gnostic origin but whose beliefs may have served better to dissociate themselves from the political control of the emperors. In 872 a military victory was won over the Paulicians and some of them were deported to the Balkans. It became the practice following this victory to try and convert the heretics. Those who withstood conversion to Catholicism may well have hot-footed it to the Balkans in the north and northwest where heresy seems to have been more easily tolerated.

In the tenth century we first hear of the Bogomil Church in Bulgaria. *Bogomil* is Bulgarian for 'beloved of God' and it may be that their founder took this name. Among their beliefs was that characteristically gnostic one which held that the Father of Jesus Christ was not the creator of the world. The Catholic Church had long held that the origin of evil for men lay in the human being's surrender to the power of the Devil. For the Bogomils and later for the Cathars, the power of the Devil worked through the nature and constraints of the material world. Since God the Father, it was believed could not have created such an evil instrument (the world, that is), it was logical to suppose that the Devil (Satanael) not only frustrated the intentions of God the Father but had constructed the stage of the world for that very purpose. It was indeed a 'wicked world'. To be bound to the world then was evil and the realization of the source of evil, coupled with the fervent desire to extricate oneself from it by virtuous practice in a religion of love and goodness, was salvation. One was redeemed to heaven by knowledge of the Good God. In short, matter and spirit were never meant to cohabit. This division and its corresponding principles of good and evil, light and darkness is broadly called dualism – the doctrine of two opposing principles between which Man is pulled.

During the early twelfth century, Bogomil missionaries began the journey up the Danube to the west, possibly as a result of the persecution of Bogomils in Constantinople. What remains a mystery is whether these Bulgarian missionaries were, in fact, the direct founders of Catharism in the Languedoc. Bogomils were burnt in Cologne in 1142 and Cologne would become a centre for Cathars in Germany. However, there were other indigenous heretics in France and it may be that Catharism developed in some sort of association with movements such as those initiated by Henry of Lausanne in the early twelfth century. Henry was profoundly moved to condemn the ecclesiastical hierarchy and the vices which went hand in hand with it, namely, wealth, power and the distance which separated that hierarchy, and thereby the knowledge of Christ, from the ordinary believer. He and others like him were branded as heretics. A heretic was somebody who felt or thought or preached that he could have a relationship with God without the authority of the

Catholic Church. What was so utterly damnable about the message of the Cathars was that not only was the Church held to be irrelevant in the matter of the soul's redemption but that the Church of Rome was positively the temple of Satan, a false church, a counterfeit produced by the Devil to outwit men and women from a true knowledge of themselves and of the work of Christ. The Church had involved itself with political power and worldly vice. Christ had said that a man cannot serve two masters: God and Money. There was among many of the nobles of Languedoc something of a consensus which held that the Church of Rome was not the kind of master worth serving – or, perhaps more importantly, worth paying for. The Catholic Church was not felt to be on their side in the 'life and death issues' of Life and Death. To those nobles and their peasants, as well as to a rising middle-class hampered by the Catholic Church's condemnation of usury, the gospel of the 'Good Men' was an alternative. The rejection of the Church of Rome by the Cathars can perhaps be seen as a response, long delayed, to the expulsion of the gnosis by the Catholics. Yet again, accusation and suspicion of licentious sexual practices was levelled at the heretics. It was quite common to hear of Cathars being described as Bulgarians or Bulgars and in England, a corruption of this word led to our word 'bugger' due to the fact that the Cathar preachers, the *parfaits* (French for 'perfects' or 'perfected ones') frequently travelled in groups of two and perhaps the popular imagination then was not so different at root from that of today.

What kind of world had Catharism entered into?

It would appear that the Bogomil missionaries arrived at just the right time. There were several major conditions operating in Languedoc which enabled Catharism to flourish. Firstly, there was a good deal of internecine strife. Land tenure was divided among a vast number of independent nobles and their families. The key word here is independent. The most powerful nobles, the Counts of Toulouse were involved in continual struggles both to annex disputed property and defend their lands and had little time to devote to interfering in the business of the territories of their allies. The Church offered a frequently poorly or non-educated, profligate clergy. Nor do the clergy seem to have been able to maintain the moral standards of their religion. At the same time, evangelism was virtually unheard of. Ignorance of the major tenets of the Catholic gospel was widespread. Meanwhile, the area gave passage to several major trade routes and there was money to be made. There were books to be bought. There was a receptivity to new ideas. Furthermore, compared to northern France, this was a good place to be a woman. Women were respected in the Languedoc and, if they were landowners or were related to the nobility, they enjoyed not only an equality but a romantic aura as well. For this was the era of the troubadours. A small Renaissance was occurring in the Languedoc and in northern Spain, a cultural effervescence at all levels with a particular regard to poetry, writing and music. Gérard Zuchetto who today lectures on the Troubadours and who sings in Occitan, the 'langue d'oc' with his acclaimed group 'Rosamonda' explains the substance of this fertile culture:

> For the first time people wrote extensively about love; courtly love, fine love, adulterous love, the love of the troubadours, and they went a long way into things. The troubadours for example were people who wrote about 'tremendous', 'inaccessible' love and respect for the lady. For the first time the lady is elevated to the level of the man and this is the most important thing in the culture and is perhaps the most symbolic thing about the cultural effervescence of the twelfth and thirteenth centuries.

Gérard believes that the Cathar *parfaite* (a woman who had passed through the Cathar 'baptism of fire' or spiritual baptism, the *Consolamentum*) may have been a romantic subject for the enamoured troubadour. The *parfaite* was chaste, was good, was spiritually pure and her heart was fixed on the divine world. In the castles of the Languedoc could be heard music from the Arab world with delicately woven words, loosening the bonds of the body and leading a fortunate nobility to love. As well as the perennial violence and threat to security, there was a 'liberal' spirit in the air. At a time when it was forbidden to write in old Provençal, when it was forbidden to think in any way other than that of the Church of Rome, 'things were written, they were sung, they were said and it was said that people needed to be free. They needed to free themselves from the tutelage of the Church, they needed to free themselves from the constraint of writing in Latin, and that was important' (Gérard Zuchetto). Dante was to write in thirteenth-century Florence that, 'It is in the Occitan language (la langue d'oc) that the exponents of the living language have made themselves the firsts (or masters) of Poesy' (*De vulgari Eloquentia*). It is highly significant that the Cathar *perfecti* made the gospels available in Occitan. This was the world in which the Cathars emerged with a message of simple spirituality. They were welcomed by many into a world which longed for purity and independence.

To those who listened, a whole world of imagination was opened and somehow, a sense of that world has come down to us. Perhaps it was 'When we were very young', when A. A. Milne wrote in *Knights and Ladies*:

> There is in my old picture book
> A page at which I like to look,
> Where knights and squires come riding down
> The cobbles of some steep old town,
> And ladies from beneath the eaves
> Flutter their bravest handkerchiefs,
> Or, smiling proudly, toss down gages ...
> But that was in the Middle Ages.
> It wouldn't happen now; but still,
> Whenever I look up the hill
> Where, dark against the green and blue,
> The firs come marching, two by two,
> I wonder if perhaps I *might*
> See suddenly a shining knight
> Winding his way from blue to green –
> Exactly as it would have been
> Those many, many years ago ...
> Perhaps I might. You never know.

We should not forget that all those persons of whom we shall hear in the following chapters were also children once – or twice.

Were the Cathars Gnostics?

In about 1172 there was held a council of Cathar *perfecti* (those who had become full or 'clothed' Cathars, having received the *Consolamentum*: baptism in the spirit by the laying on of hands). It took place at a house in S. Félix-de-Caraman about 30 kilometres from Toulouse. Presided over by a Bogomil bishop from Constantinople, Nicetas, it planned the strategy for presenting the 'true' Christianity to the people of the Languedoc. It represented a major bid for a revised organization of the Cathar Church and for the supplanting of the Catholic Church by the power of the Holy Spirit and by the oratory of its leaders. We may ask, 'Was Languedoc in the process of receiving gnosticism?' Professor Bernard Hamilton of Nottingham University in his paper *The Albigensian Crusade* (page 6. *The Historical Association*. G.85) has written that:

Catharism was not a form of gnosticism, teaching salvation by knowledge: like Catholicism, it was a profoundly sacramental faith. The Cathars taught that Christ had given his Church a single sacrament, the *consolamentum*, baptism in the spirit by the laying-on of hands. This differed from the Catholic sacrament of confirmation, for the spirit which was conferred by the Cathar rite was not God the Holy Spirit but the recipient's own spirit.

Professor Hamilton is obviously mistaken as to the multi-faceted nature of gnosticism. If gnosticism was truly a religion 'teaching salvation by knowledge' then it would be pertinent to ask of the nature of such knowledge. A classic definition of gnostic 'knowledge' has long been furnished in Clement of Alexandria's *Excerpta ex Theodoto* (second century): 'the knowledge of who we were, and what we have become, where we were or into what we have been thrown, whither we hasten, from what we are redeemed'.

This was precisely what the Cathar *perfecti* did teach. They taught that the souls of angelic beings had been stolen by 'Sathanas' and put into the bodies of men which he had made in his own likeness, whence came the yearning for the realm of pure spirit enjoyed prior to the rebellious acts of Sathanas. As it is written in the Cathar *Les Questions de Jean*:

> And he [Satan] imagined in order to make man for his service, and took the lime of the earth and made man in his resemblance. And he ordered the angel of the second heaven to enter into the body of lime; and he took another part and made another body in the form of woman, and he ordered the angel of the first heaven to enter therein. The angels cried exceedingly on seeing themselves covered in distinct forms by this mortal envelopment.

The author of the work goes on to recount how Sathanas made Paradise for the purpose of making the 'man' and 'woman' sin. He accomplished his malicious purpose and so further held the angelic souls in bondage. The rite of *consolamentum*, the 'enspiriting' of the Cathar effectively released the soul from the grip of the Devil's material bondage and united it with the spirit of God, the Holy Spirit, which until the rite exists, as it were, in a dormant state attending the delivery made possible by the love of Christ. The *perfectus* could now, in all truth call God 'Father'. As Hamilton rightly says, it is the recipient's own spirit that is released from the hell or further incarnations or embodiments. The *perfectus* is thus able to love without fear and, as attachment to the material world (governed by Satan the *Rex Mundi* or King of the World) declines, the spirit of the Cathar is able to reach in love for the final departure from the body and the reception into heaven. Since the world, being an inferior and unspiritual creation, had a limited duration; since it was in a profound sense an unreal world, the perfected Cathar thus passed from non-being into the realm of Being. The Cathar was in the Light. The *Consolamentum* was, like the Valentinian ἀπολυτρωσις (apolytrosis meaning redemption) a liberation sacrament. The perfected one *knew*.

I asked the respected French historian of Catharism, Michel Rocquebert, who himself now lives in the village of Montsegur in the Ariège, whether there was a gnosis in Catharism. His reply was clear enough:

Undeniably. The idea that there are two creations and therefore two creators; one good creation and one bad creation; the idea that the soul which belongs to the good creation is an exile and prisoner of the world, that is to say, of the bad creation; the idea that salvation can only be achieved by illuminative knowledge, all that is gnostic. But it should not be forgotten that Catharism is a form of Christianity, and has always presented itself as being a form of Christianity, even as being true Christianity. So we are dealing with an undeniably gnostic form of Christianity, and that is why, moreover, I am personally convinced that Catharism did not appear by a miracle right in the middle of the Middle Ages in the eleventh and twelfth centuries, but that in actual fact the origins of Catharism should be sought in primitive Christianity.

Prior to moving on to the next chapter which reveals aspects of the so-called Albigensian Crusade we should consider the following. The Cathars believed that the Church of Rome was of the nature of the *Rex Mundi*, the Lord of this world. To the Cathar Gnostic, the incidence and nature of the Albigensian Crusade shows precisely what he meant.

Chapter Five

A Mystery Tour

It might be a good idea to explore the world of the Cathars and their eventual fate in the manner of a tour, a kind of mystery tour. We shall take a trip into the heartlands of Catharism as it existed from the late twelfth century to the mid-thirteenth century. So let us cast our minds and imaginations back some 800 years.

Laurac

We begin our journey high up in the rugged hills of Laurac, some 25 kilometres to the west of Carcassonne, our central reference point.

We are standing on a promontory just above a squat and simple church. The promontory is a defensive position and it commands a spectacular view of undulating green hills and golden strips of corn which take our eyes across the vast plain before us to the misty horizons of the northwest, north and northeast. The wood and stone town huddles together on the hillside all about us. Behind us, in extreme contrast, the hills have the character of moorland and scrub, casting dark shadows about a dull green and brown. Beyond those hills, far to the south exists a powerful threat to the Counts of Toulouse who claim this place and its surrounding country as their own. For beyond the Pyrenees the kings of Aragon and the counts of Barcelona also claim this land. Between these two powers are the counts of Foix, vassals of the king of Aragon, and the viscounts of Carcassonne and Béziers, the Trencavel family who are fiercely attempting to maintain control of their lands. Laurac is a Trencavel outpost.

Sometime in the middle of the twelfth century the Cathars began to appear. In spite of spectacular landscapes, which doubtless please us more than the population of the time, it would not be so difficult to think these lands to be the work of the Devil. A Papal Legate, Stephen of Tournai came to these parts in 1181 and wrote of 'vast deserts ruled by the fury of brigands and the image of death; of burned houses and

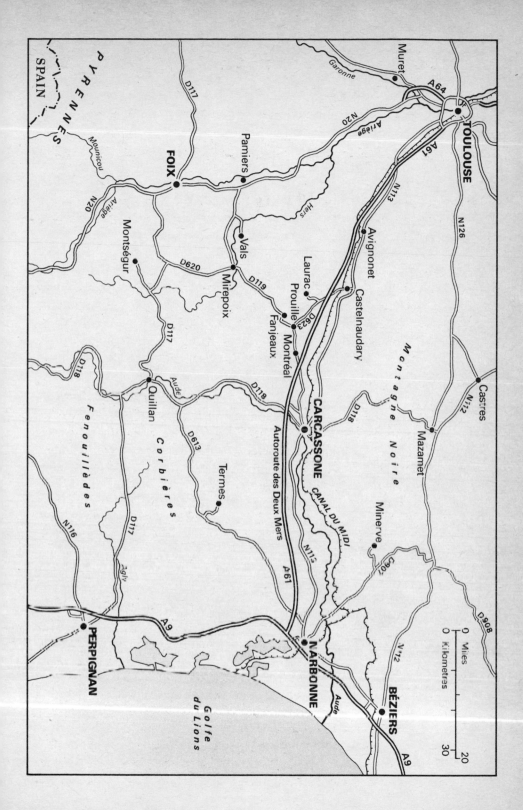

ruined villages where there is no order, no tranquillity, nothing that does not threaten security and menace life itself'. At the same time as punitive raids were conducted by a ferocious array of mercenary soldiers there was a good deal of trade passing through these lands, for if we could see far enough to the east we should see the Mediterranean and, to the northwest, the trading centre of Bordeaux and the Atlantic. The lords of Laurac, of which there were many, wanted their share of this trade and indeed, if you were working in the fields of the plain below or travelling through the country laden with goods and money, you might well look up at Laurac and feel a sense of menace.

To this situation the Cathars came with a message which held that not only was the world of matter evil but that the worst form of expression of that evil could be seen in the exercise of power and above all, the violent exercise of power. The Cathars held out the possibility of another way of life which would be characterized by freedom from fear. The discovery of the spiritual light within the believing Cathar removed him or her from the grip of the Devil and of the Devil's servants. In order to purify oneself and so prepare for the eternal realm of spirit from which one had come, it was necessary to abstain from sex because you thereby risked dragging down another immortal soul into this hell, and from meat, because meat was the Devil's matter and was the product of procreation – as was milk, and from all those sins or temptations whereby the Devil could get a hold on you. You must not lie or kill people or animals because, well, who knew whether there was in that animal a pained soul working through successive incarnations in order to return to heaven? You must not hate. In short, you must love as Christ had loved. Not all Cathars had to adhere to these 'rules'. There were *crédentes*, believers who revered the Cathar *perfecti* but who preferred to leave the final break with the world – the *Consolamentum* – to their deathbeds, or, in the case of women, until after they had raised families when the pain was almost over and they could embrace that holy life which was to win the *parfaite* almost universal respect in this region.

The English historian R.I. Moore has shed further light on the vegetarianism of the Cathars:

> I think another thing about not eating meat which gave it a social power as a spiritual message, and it was a message which was preached not only by Cathars but by other religions which opposed Catholic orthodoxy in this period, was that meat was the food of the hunters, of the dominators, of the people who rode horses, the people who exploited the cultivators of the land, most of whose life was singularly meatless.

Listening to the Cathar *perfecti* no doubt gave the lords of Laurac release from the pressing demands on their arms and pockets. For a moment they might begin to believe there was a way out of all the troubles. Most importantly, anyone who has travelled about Europe and marvelled at the immense grandeur of her churches, abbeys and cathedrals can be in no doubt that concern for the fate of the soul was intense. To those who had become cynical of the Catholic Church or who had never been convinced, to those who sought answers which spoke of their experience of life and their dreams of heaven, to these people the Cathars spoke. They were rewarded with patronage and, eventually, by a loyalty unto death.

Soon the Cathars had houses in Laurac where the *perfecti* lived and which served as centres and refuges as they went about the country consoling the willing believer and helping out with the day's toil.

Fanjeaux

Imagine a wintry afternoon in February 1190. You have been invited to stay at a weaver's house in Fanjeaux about two hours' walk away. You descend the hill from Laurac down to the soft hills below and head southeast. These hills weave among each other and bind your world as the illuminations of a manuscript enclose the daily prayer. There are no labourers in the fields now and the tops of the hills turn from a brilliant wet turquoise to a pink glow and then, as it becomes colder and the wind scurries from hedge to hedge, the world becomes grey. Soon it will be almost black. A crescent moon hovers behind some dark cloud and you are in starlight with only the stars and the approaching fires of Fanjeaux to guide you. You struggle up the hill to the town. A bell booms out from the depths of the high church tower and echoes about the narrow streets. You walk through the empty market-place, avoiding the standing rough-hewn beams which support its roof and come to a stone house. The thick wooden door creaks open and you are welcomed into the flickering fire-light. There about the fire are the silhouettes of men and women quietly talking. These are the *parfaits* and the *parfaites* engaging in talk about the week's events. The atmosphere is very good. You are among the good spirits now and you can relax with a mug of wine and listen ...

This weaver's shop is one of several in Fanjeaux, the heart of Catharism. In 1246, a man called Pierre Gramazie told the Inquisitors that he had grown up as a boy in Fanjeaux and worked in a weaver's shop which was kept by *perfecti*. These houses were often given for their use by local lords who were themselves not very removed from the ordinary townsfolk. They did not have much money. We know that the Cathars also set up cobblers shops and potteries in the area. We know of two Cathar doctors who practised in Fanjeaux. The Cathars did not worship in churches. The place of prayer, worship and discussion was not important. They said: 'The church of God is not made of stone or wood; it is the community of the faithful.'

This view is characteristic of the gnostic belief in an invisible 'ekklesia' or 'assembly' of souls who know one another 'by heart'. Madame Anne Brenon, director of the Centre Nationale d'études Cathares in Villegly near to Carcassonne told me that, 'In the days when followers of Catharism were not persecuted, their place of worship might have been a room in a château or a room in an inn. When they came to be persecuted, their place of worship might have been a clearing in a wood, or in a cave or cellar.' In Fanjeaux, where there were at least fifty lords, one of them, Dame Cavaers, presided over a Cathar house and this was not at all unusual. Blanche de Tonneins we know also held a Cathar house near Fanjeaux at the Motte de Tonneins. In 1206, Esclarmonde of Foix, the sister of the Count of Foix received the *Consolamentum* here at a ceremony attended also by a great lord of Fanjeaux, her brother Raymond-Roger and which was conducted by the most famous Cathar *parfait*, Guilhabert de Castres. Indeed, the role of women was of primary importance in Catharism. Perhaps it is that women become more interested in a spiritual religion than men, at least to begin with. That was the case in the Languedoc. The noble women were the first to be touched by the Cathar message and, according to Anne Brenon:

One has the impression that there was a whole generation of Cathar matriarchs who directed the thought of three or four generations of their lineage. I am thinking of ladies like Blanche de Laurac, like the lady of Le Mas Saintes Puelles, Garsyne, and this is explained by the fact that the Cathar religion gave women just as important a role to play in the spiritual movement, whereas the Catholic religion [and the northern barons] relegated women to the level of simple enclosed nuns when they were allowed to take holy orders. In Catharism, on the other hand, female *perfecti* were the equal of male *perfecti*. They were entitled to preach, like men; they were also entitled to confer the sacrament which they had received (the *Consolamentum*); they had an important spiritual role. And when one thinks that women in the Languedoc at this time in history – at least women who belonged to the nobility – also had their say in matters of relations between men and women, matters of love. There is a certain logic to be found in all that.

Dame Cavaers provided for a *parfait* to teach her daughter and it seems that many of the *parfaites* came from noble families with high spiritual intent. The holiness and perfection to which the Cathars aspired existed beyond sexual differences. According to the theory, the *Consolamentum* ensured that further sinfulness, whether connected with sex or another kind, was out of the question. If, however, the prohibitions which ensured sanctity were broken, the *Consolamentum* ceased to operate and might only be performed again in extraordinary circumstances. Furthermore, if a *parfait* sinned, all those who had received the *Consolamentum* from him or her would also have to be reconsoled. It is little wonder that many Cathars waited until they were dying before entering the full redemption. As the Jesus of the Nag Hammadi Library says, 'This is the doctrine for the perfect.' Catharism was unlikely then to be a real threat to the social order of the Languedoc. Nevertheless, it was very much seen that way.

In 1179 Pope Alexander III pronounced the Cathars to be anathema, that is, to put it bluntly, burnable. From then on the Cathars of the Languedoc were a priority target for the Catholic authorities. Nevertheless, the Catholic bishops who initially attempted to deal with Catharism were unable to muster a concerted effort due to conflicting diocesan initiatives and the unwillingness of the Languedoc nobility to persecute their own countrymen. In 1203, Peter of Castelnau became a Papal Legate and he together with the ruthlessly authoritarian Arnaud Amaury, Abbot of Citeaux and founder of the Cistercian order of which Peter of Castelnau was a monk, took to the roads of the region to convince Cathars of their folly and to persuade the nobility of their responsibilities to the Church of Christ. In 1204, there was a confrontation between Cathar leaders and the Papal Legates in Carcassonne. The contrasting postures of the protagonists led one observer to exclaim that, 'Here was a God who always went on foot – yet today his servants ride in comfort. Here was a God of poverty – yet today his missionaries are wealthy. Here was a God humble and scorned of men – yet today his envoys are loaded with honours.'

It was in perhaps the same year as this abortive attempt at winning the Cathars over by oratory that Raymond de Péreille, seigneur of Puivert, began the reconstruction of the fortress of Montségur at the request of local Cathars. It would serve as an administrative centre, as a refuge and as a treasury for the funds that were being donated by the seigneurial class. Perhaps, somehow, they knew what was coming.

Enter Dominic Guzman

Dominic Guzman (*circa* 1172–1221) was on his way back from a mission to Denmark with Diego, Bishop of Osma in Castile in 1204–5. Today we know him as St Dominic, founder of the Dominican Order. In many places Roman Catholic children learn of this man's holiness. What was he like in those days?

Dominic Guzman was born in Caleruaga in Castile to an aristocratic family. His mother was of the d'Aza family and she is known to have been deeply religious and very charitable. The d'Aza family had served the Church by its military exploits against the Moorish infidel. The family had good connections and Dominic joined the cathedral chapter of Osma as an Augustinian canon. He showed himself to be a deeply compassionate man, a highly effective orator and good in argument. He tried to relieve the lot of the poor. He sold his books and manuscripts declaring, 'I will not study on dead skins while men are dying of hunger'. He was given to the mortification of the flesh and flogged himself – a not uncommon practice among Catholic mystics and serious clerics. His thin stature and uncertain health were not assisted by his frequently staying up all night weeping for those he tried so hard to convert. His successor as Head of the Dominicans (founded in 1215) Jordan of Saxony wrote of him: 'God had given him a special grace to weep for sinners and for the afflicted and oppressed. He bore their distress in the inmost shrine of his compassion.' Dominic wanted to give himself totally to the end of winning souls for Christ: 'his heart was full of an extraordinary, almost incredible yearning for the salvation of everyone'.

His attitude to heretics in general was, however, severe. They were worse than the infidel. This conviction was doubtless an influence of his having been brought up in a part of Castile but recently reconquered from the Moorish empire of Almohad. The territory gained for Christ was insecurely held. Christianity was under attack from without. Perhaps there is a parallel here with the situation of Bishop Irenaeus in the second century who also experienced Christianity under attack from without and who would give the gnostic threat from within short shrift. For Dominic, the heretics were a kind of 'fifth column' attacking the very foundations of Catholic life. For him, heresy attacked God (it denied He was Creator), Truth (it denied the Catholic Church) and so the whole structure of Catholic society was undermined by it. Heresy hit Church and State. In the Languedoc neither Church nor State was yet particularly strong. One would be mistaken if one thought that Dominic was interested in a witch-hunt for the sake of it. Heresy he detested, but the treatment of individual heretics was another matter. He longed to convert them. However, given the choice, he preferred the full challenge of converting the heathen. In 1204, on his way to Rome, he encountered heresy in Toulouse. The host of the inn in which he stayed was a Cathar. Dominic stayed up all night in argument with him and won him round. He could still think of a heretic as a Christian who had gone astray. In 1205, he and Diego went to Rome and asked permission of the Pope, Innocent III, for the Bishop of Osma to resign his episcopal duties so that he and Dominic might return northwards in order to convert the pagans recently made visible by the expansion of the Teutonic knights of Prussia and the Nordic countries. Dominic was a born evangelist. Nevertheless, the Pope refused the request. Innocent III had recently been alerted to the Dualist heresies of Bosnia and Bulgaria over which he was now Pope and he feared the international dimensions of the heresy. The Albigensian problem had to be dealt with first, and quickly. In 1206 Dominic was put under the authority of the Legates Arnaud Amaury and Peter of Castelnau so as to accomplish what they had failed to do. Dominic was, in a sense, the Pope's last card. While Dominic went around the Languedoc with a new strategy – renouncing the accoutrements of wealth and power, wearing simple clothes, walking barefoot, sleeping by the roadside and in many things playing the *perfecti* at their own game – a greater game continued above him. Peter of Castlenau was putting great pressure on Raymond VI, Count of Toulouse, to invade the Trencavel territories to destroy the Cathar heresy. In retrospect, the mission of Dominic makes him appear as a political stooge.

Dominic came to Fanjeaux where, taking in the scope of his task while gazing from the heights of this fair town, he experienced a revelation and decided to make the nearby village of Prouille his base. By doing so Dominic was to become party to a truly historic confrontation. Fanjeaux, at this time, was the base of the greatest Cathar preacher of the era, a man both famous and highly respected, Guilhabert de Castres. We know a good deal about his long career but, sadly, not much about the man.

Guilhabert de Castres (circa 1150–1240)

I asked Anne Brenon to provide a portrait of the man. It is tantalizingly incomplete.

> Guilhabert de Castres was one of the most famous Cathar doctors in the polite society of the Lauragais and Carcassès (region of Carcassonne). He certainly originated from Castres (northeast of Toulouse), no doubt

from the noble family of de Castres. He was certainly someone of good birth and having attained his majority, he very soon attracted the attention of the Cathar 'Bishop' (called so by the Catholic enemy) of Toulouse and as *filius major* (the bishop's 'elder son') he chose to take up residence in Fanjeaux which was, in fact, the town which the troubadour Peire Vidal portrayed as the centre of *courtoisie* (courtly love) in this region, but which was also the centre of the heresy. Fanjeaux was a nobility town where people conversed a great deal. Guilhabert de Castres exercised a ministry there for twenty years before taking up residence at Montségur; at a time, moreover, when there was persecution and virtually the whole of the polite society of Fanjeaux had also emigrated to Montségur. Although of noble birth and a formidable Cathar intellectual jouster against Catholic jousters, Guilhabert de Castres nevertheless had a fervent apostolate among all the ordinary Cathar people.

This man sounds fascinating. What else do we know about him? Suzanne Nélli, (widow of the late historian and philosopher of Catharism, René Nélli) believes that it is likely that this man was the same abbot Guilhabert de Castres who was sent by Raymond VI, Count of Toulouse as Ambassador to Richard I of England, the Lion Heart. Already in 1178 the Pope had sent a mission to the region of Castres, the latter place having the reputation for being 'a receptacle of heretics' and it is there that we first hear of a *Bonus Homo de Castris* – a Good Man of Castres.

In 1219, Guilhabert 'held house' at Dun with Raimond Mercier the Cathar deacon of Mirepoix, in the same château in which Philippa de Foix ran a house of *parfaites* in 1206 and to which Guilhabert would return several years later with Bernard de Lamothe and Guiraud de Gourdon in order to 'console' Raymond d'Avigna, the seigneur (lord) of Dun. All of them just names to us now.

In the same year, Guilhabert was again seen at Montségur where he consoled Guillaume de Latour de Laurac. From 1220 he was the leader of the Cathar diocese of Toulouse and his tireless ministry extended from there to as far south as Usson and Sabarthès in the lower Ariège some 80 kilometres south of Fanjeaux. In those years he visited the houses of *parfaits* and *parfaites*, preaching, blessing, consoling – in Fanjeaux, Laurac, Montréal, Blesplas, Castelnaudary, Labécède-Lauragais, Villeneuve-la-Comptal, Le Mas Saintes Puelles, Toulouse, Saint-Paul-Cap-de-Joux, Lanta, Castres, Mirepoix, Foix, Miramont de Sabarthès, le Bézu, Dourne, Rocquefeuil, Usson and in the castles and houses of the Cathar aristocrats, and then, perhaps finally, at Montségur.

Suzanne Nélli writes that: 'He appears to us as a man of destiny, the

The Cathars were great orators with a message both simple and direct. Guilhabert de Castres (Brian Blessed) preaching at Laurac.

Dominic Guzman lived in this house at Fanjeaux.

The Church at Vals.

The Château of Montségur which fell in 1244.

The Church of Santa Maria Novella as seen by a Florentine artist in 1460 – the year in which the Corpus Hermeticum arrived at the court of Cosimo de Medici. (From the Ms. Holkham. Misc. 49. Boccacchio. Folio No. 5. Bodleian Library, Oxford.)

The Hermetic Dialogue of Asclepius was known before the arrival of the Greek *Corpus Hermeticum* in 1460. An extract from this work was discovered among the books of the Nag Hammadi Library. It was customary to include the work among the *opera* of Lucius Apuleius. This copy was printed in 1488.

IN LATINVM CONVERSIO

HERMETIS TRIMEGISTI DIALOGVS LVT. APV / LEII MADAVRENSIS PHILOSOPHI PLATONICI IN LATINVM CONVERSIO.

Sclepius iste pro sole mihi est deus Deus te no/
bis o Asclepi:ut diuino smoni interesses: addu/
xit:eiq; tali:q merito omniū antea a nobis facto
ruᵐ. uel nobis diuino munere ispiratoᵣ: uidea/
tur eē religiosa pietate diuinior:quē si itelligēs
uideris:eris omniū bonoᵣ tota mēte pleissimᵒ.
Sed cū multa sint bona: & nō unū:i quo sūt oia
alteᵣ.n.alteriᵒ cōsentaneū esse dinoscit:oia unius esse:aut unum esse
oia.Ita.n.unū alteri cōnexū:ut separari alteᵣ ab utroq3 nō possit.S3
de futuro smone hoc diligēti intentiōe cognosces. Tu uero o Ascle/
pi pcede paululū:atq3 nobis:q iter sit:euoca.   Quo ingresso:Ascle
pius etiam Ammonē iterecñ suggessit.   Trimegistus ait:nulla in/
uidia Ammonē phibet a nobis:eteni ad eiᵒ nomē multa meminimus
a nobis esse scripta:sicut & ad amantissimū & bonū filium:multa de
physica:& ex ethica qplurima:tractatū hunc aūt tuo ascribaᵌ nomi
ni:præter Ammonē uero nullum uoca alteᵣ:ne tanta rei religiosissi/
mus sermo multorū interuentu ueniētium:præsentiaq3 uiolet : tra/
ctᵃᵗᵘm aūt tota numinis maiestate plenissimū irreligiosæ mētis est:
multorum conscientiæ publicare. Ammone etiam aditum ingresso:
sanctoq3 illo:quattuor uirorum religione:& diuino dei cōpletu præ
sentia:competenti uenerabiliter silentio ex ore Hermes animis singu/
lorū mentibusq3 pendentibᵒ : diuinus Cupido sic exorsus est dicere.
.TRIMEGISTVS.   O Asclepi omnis humana immortalis
est anima:sed non uniformiter cuncta:sed alia alio more:uel tempo/
re. .ASCLEPIVS.   Non enim o Trimegiste omnis uniᵒ qua/
litatis est anima. .TRIME.   O Asclepi: ut celeriter de uera ra/
tionis continentia didicisti. Non enim hoc dixi : omnia unum esse:
& unum omnia : ut quæ i creatore sunt omnia:anteq creasset omnia:
nec immerito ipse dictus est omnia: cuius membra sunt omnia:huiᵒ
itaque qui est unus omnia : uel ipse est creator omnium:in hac una
disputatione curato meminisse : de cælo cuncta descendunt in terra:
& in aquam : & in aera . Ignis solum : q sursum uersum fertur :
uiuificat : quod deorsum ei deseruiens: at uero quicquid de alto de/
scendit : generans est : quod sursū uersus emanat nutriens,terra sola

Hermes comes to Florence. This is part of the original manuscript of the *Corpus Hermeticum* brought to Florence in 1460 from Macedonia by Leonardo of Pistoia. It now resides in the Bibliotheca Medicea Laurentiana in Florence.

MERCVRII TRISMEGISTI LIBER DE POTESTATE ET SAPIENTIA DEI E GRAECO IN LATINVM TRADVCTVS A MARSILIO FICINO FLORENTINO AD COSMVM MEDICEM PATRIAE PATREM. PIMANDER INCIPIT.

Vm de rerum natura cogita,
rem:ac mentis aciem ad sup,
na erigere:sopitis iam corpis
sensibus:quemadmodum ac,
cidere solet iis:qui ob saturitatem:uel defa
tigationem:somno grauati sunt.subito mihi
uisus sum cernere quédam:immensa magni
tudine corporis:qui me nomine uocans:in
húc modum clamaret. Quid est o Mercuri:
quod et audire:et intueri desideras? Quid
est:quod discere atq; intelligere cupis? Tu
ego:quisnam es inq̃? Sum inquit ille Piman
der mens diuinæ potentiæ.at tu uide:quid
uelis.ipse uero tibi ubiq; adero.Cupio iquã
rerum naturam discere.deumq; cognoscere.
Ad hæc ille.Tua me méte complectere:&

'Alice in Egypt.' Marsilio Ficino's translation of the *Pymander* for Cosimo de Medici. Mercurius Trismegistus is described as a contemporary of Moses and of Atlas 'the astrologer'. It is now in the Bibliotheca Medicea Laurentiana.

The first printed version of Ficino's translation of the *Pymander*, 1471.

Hermes inspires Giovanni Pico della Mirandola. The *Oratio* or Oration on the Dignity of Man. Pico quotes from *Asclepius*: 'A great miracle, O Asclepius, is man,' in his 1486 preface to 900 Theses. This version was printed in Venice in 1498.

Dr John Dee as portrayed in *A true and faithful relation of what passed for many years between Dr John Dee and some spirits*, with a preface by Meric Casaubon, London 1659.

HENRICVS CORNELIVS AGRIPPA.

Henry Cornelius Agrippa of Nettesheim as he appears in an edition of *De Occulta Philosophia*, published in Köln by Johann Söter in 1533.

GIORDA-
NO BRVNO
Nolano.

De la caufa, principio, et Vno.

A' L' Illuftriſsimo Signor di Mauuiſsiero.

Stampato in Venetia.
Anno. M. D. LXXXIIII.

Giordano Bruno the Nolan, *Of the Cause, the Principle and the One*, published not in Venice as stated but in London, perhaps for political reasons. Bruno was living at the French Embassy in London at the time.

QVI NON INTELLIGIT, AVT TACEAT, AVT DISCAT.

MONAS HIEROGLYPHICA
IOANNIS DEE, LONDINENSIS,
AD
MAXIMILIANVM, DEI GRATIA
ROMANORVM, BOHEMIÆ ET HVNGARIÆ
REGEM SAPIENTISSIMVM.

IGNIS · AER

DE RORE CÆLI, ET PINGVEDINE TERRÆ, DET TIBI DEVS. Gen.27.
Guliel.Silvius Typog.Regius, Excud.Antuerpiæ, 1564.

The *Monas Hieroglyphica* of John Dee, published in Antwerp in 1564. The Latin inscription on the portal tells the reader that if he does not understand the contents he ought to seek understanding or keep his mouth shut.

IORDANVS
BRVNVS NOLANVS
DE VMBRIS IDEARVM.

Implicantibus artem, Quærendi, Inueniendi, Iudicandi, Ordinandi, & Applicandi:

Ad internam ſcripturam, & non vulgares per memoriam operationes explicatis.

AD HENRICVM III. SEREniſ. Gallor. Polonorúmque Regem,&c.

PROTESTATIO.

Vmbra profunda ſumus, né nos vexetis inepti.
Non vos, ſed doctes tam graue quærit opus.

Bruno's *Of the Shadows of Ideas*, which deals in part with his Art of Memory which was influenced by Hermetic concepts.

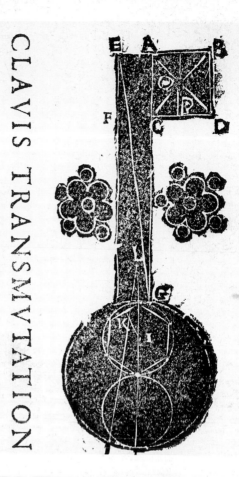

CLAVIS TRANSMVTATION

'The Key of Transmutation' from *De triplici minimo et mensura*. The book contains ideas for a primitive and magical form of atomic physics.

Joseph Ritman, Gnostic man of Business, in the offices of *de Ster*, Amsterdam. Behind him, Hermes points the way: 'God is an infinite sphere whose centre is everywhere, circumference nowhere.'

Bibliotheca Philosophica Hermetica, Amsterdam: the old library (*above*), and the new library (*below*).

man chosen and protected by destiny, the kind of man that history sometimes presents us with.'

We do not know when he died. Some have thought he died during the seige of Montségur but there is no evidence to support this. He might have died a natural death there but, bearing in mind his fame, it is surprising that there is no reference to this within the copious records of the Inquisition. Perhaps he was removed, notwithstanding his great age, from Montségur, to be hidden away in the castle of a sympathetic noble. Perhaps it is right that such a mysterious man should leave us guessing as to the nature of his final departure from this world.

The Debates

In the year 1207 Guilhabert de Castres and Dominic Guzman faced each other at Montréal, a small town about two hours' walk in a northeasterly direction from Fanjeaux. They did so before a local audience who were doubtless given to cheering-on their 'favourite'. On the other hand these were very serious affairs and debate could become hard and bitter. We do not know what passed between Dominic and Guilhabert. That is a great pity. We only need look at their respective careers to know that this must have been one of the great moments or 'happenings' before the troops came carrying the torch and the cross. In the Channel 4 series 'The Gnostics' there is a dramatic encounter set in Fanjeaux which I wrote to give some imaginary idea of what such a debate might have consisted of. The protagonists get off to a fine start:

GUILHABERT: Welcome Dominic to Fanjeaux! You have good news for us?

DOMINIC: That is a matter entirely in your hands – your having repeatedly rejected the gracious hand of God.

GUILHABERT: Are you the hand of God Dominic? Or the hand of the Pope?

DOMINIC: The sword of God is sharp and has two sides, Guilhabert de Castres. But it is one sword.

GUILHABERT: You speak of the sword of God, Papal Envoy. For men it *is* different. He who lives by the sword shall die by the sword so speaks the Master – not in Rome but in Heaven!

As played by the actors Brian Blessed and Ian Brooker it was a fine contest. But what were these debates really all about? It was common practice in this region to hold a public debate in order to expose and contest disputed positions of theology and philosophy. This was what politics was thought to be all about. For the Catholic Legates they were something of a shock. In 1178 a Papal Legate had been outraged to find himself granting passes of safe-conduct so that self-confessed heretics might come to Toulouse and debate openly with him. The nobility in particular must have enjoyed the spectacle immensely – the sight of priests having to prove the 'truth' of the Catholic position. And publicly at that. The Cathars were formidable opponents because they appealed less to the mysteries of The Church and more to commonsense and experience of life. In one debate the Cathar *parfait* said that if the hosts used in the Mass were truly the Body of Christ, then if all the hosts were gathered together, it would be found that Christ had a body as big as a mountain! The Cathars believed that Christ was a wholly spiritual being and he was not to be identified with the body he appeared in. Thus, they were sickened by the sight of the bleeding Jesus nailed to a cross, especially when this was used as a religious image. The Resurrection and the Ascension of Jesus were the critical events of his life because they were seen as events of the spirit, not of the flesh. The Crucifixion only served to demonstrate the blindness and cruelty of *Rex Mundi* and his servants. There was a debate in Pamiers where, during a heated moment, Esclarmonde of Foix (consoled as you remember by Guilhabert de Castres amid the great gathering of lords in Fanjeaux in 1206) got up to make a point only to be 'put down' by Brother Étienne de la Misericorde with the words: 'Madame, go back to your distaff – it does not become you to speak at such gatherings.'

This shocking remark scandalized the assembled throng. Was it because she was a woman wanting to speak – a perfectly acceptable thing for the public, or, was it because the remark implied that the sister of the Count of Foix, a holy lady, worked for a living?

The historian R. I. Moore of Sheffield has put this matter of outrage at public debate in a nutshell: '... that openness and that lack of hierarchy and structure here was something which was particularly appalling for men who had spent their lives in England, in France and in the Roman Church constructing a hierarchical, authoritarian world which gave them security.'

Failing as he did to convert the Cathars in any but the smallest numbers, Dominic must have felt a great burden of sadness. He carried on. His most important tactic was to found a convent at Prouille which offered a direct alternative to the houses where the *parfaites* lived, worked and prayed. It became a centre for a Catholic mission for evangelical and pastoral labour and it exists to this day. Guilhabert watched on. Perhaps he laughed. Perhaps he was melancholy to find such a good man as Dominic on the 'other side'. What, he may have pondered, had kept them apart?

It was at Prouille that Dominic was reported as having made the following speech to an assembly of Cathars:

> For several years now I have spoken words of peace to you. I have preached to you; I have besought you with tears. But as the common saying goes in Spain: where a blessing fails, a good thick stick will succeed. Now we shall rouse princes and prelates against you; and they, alas, will in their turn assemble whole nations and peoples, and a mighty number will perish by the sword. Towers will fall, and walls will be razed to the ground, and you will all of you be reduced to servitude. Thus force will prevail where gentle persuasion has failed to do so.

By 1208, Dominic's mission had, in its grandest aspects, ended. It was left for others to bear the 'thick stick'. During the previous year, Peter of Castelnau had clashed with Raymond VI, Count of Toulouse. Raymond had refused to join a projected league of southern barons dedicated to the task of hunting for the heretics. Peter of Castelnau excommunicated him. On 15 January 1208, Peter of Castelnau was, following the Becket precedent, cut down by officers of Raymond's army while crossing the Rhone at St. Gilles in Provence. Pope Innocent III seized this opportunity to issue a call to arms.

The weaving days were almost over.

Minerve

In the summer of 1209 an army was assembled in Lyon consisting of about 10,000 men and as many camp followers. The army had been collected from all over northern Europe and included Bretons, Flemings, Lorrainers, people from Cologne, from the coast of the Baltic and doubtless some from England too. Its commanders included the Bishops of Chartres and of Beauvais. In supreme command apart from Christ – for whom the Crusade was officially undertaken – was Simon de Montfort, either an extremely fervent Catholic and defender of Mother Church or an avaricious religious bigot, depending on your point of view. At his right hand, or rather before him, administering the sacraments and the policy of Rome was the Papal Legate Arnaud Amaury. The army quickly moved upon the city of Béziers and its citizens. In a legendary remark, Amaury responded to the question: 'How shall we tell who are the heretics?' with the answer, 'Kill them all, the Lord will know his own.' The remark, legendary as it undoubtedly is expresses the 'spirit' of the Albigensian Crusade.

About 40 kilometres northeast of Carcassonne, in the region of the Causse exists an extraordinary natural feature. After travelling through acre after acre of vineyard you are aware of reaching a high plateau. Holmoak trees are dotted about here and there but mostly the land is bare and rather rough. Stones and rocks are strewn about and a slight breeze blows little clouds of chalky substance into the air. All of a sudden the plateau opens out into a deep gorge which becomes wider and wider as you pass along it. Taking a bend in the gorge you may be astonished to see it divide. The channels of the gorge have twisted around a hard rock 'island' which, if you could see it from the air is shaped like a long apostrophe and on it is the fortified town of Minerve. Had you seen the place in the summer of 1210 as the Crusaders did, you would have seen the sides of the 'island' encrusted with battlements and breach defences. Behind these were the layers of houses, sandy brown dwellings with those familiar mottled and ruddy roofs. Near the centre of the town is the church, of such a simplicity, size and shape that we might call it a chapel. At the narrow end of the apostrophe and then opening out to form something of an 'exclamation mark' stood the castle. Of this castle only a single supporting buttress now remains. In the June of 1210 there was no water in the gorge and so the defenders, led by Guillaume, Viscount of Minerve, were totally dependent on the town well. Since the chances of taking the town by scaling the sides of the gorges (about five thick layers of sediment climbing to about 70 metres) were poor, Simon de Montfort took advantage instead of the latest siege technology. The queen of this technology went by the jocular name of *Malevoisine* (bad neighbour) and had been designed specially for the Crusade by the engineer William of Paris. De Montfort had her set up at the edge of the plateau nearest to the town from where she commenced the medieval equivalent of massive aerial bombardment. In spite of a setback when 'commandos' from the town set her alight, the alarm was sounded and the trebuchet, the great missile-throwing engine, continued the attack. The well was sealed and as the parching summer continued, the defence of Minerve began to take a downward turn. Five weeks after the commencement of the siege, Guillaume de Minerve had to sue for peace.

An arrangement was come to whereby all those who were Catholic or who surrendered the Cathar faith would be set free. At this, many of the soldiers baulked. They had not come all that way, they said, to watch heretics go free. They had come to exterminate them. Arnaud Amaury felt himself to be in a cleft stick. As a chronicler put it: 'He passionately desired to see God's enemies die. But as a priest and monk he must not dare to strike the blow himself.' Anyhow, he replied to the disgruntled officers, 'Don't worry. They won't recant.'

He was quite right. Simon de Montfort and Arnaud Amaury led the way into the town behind a cross which was borne as far as the church. De Montfort and Amaury then went knocking on the doors of the town inviting the Cathar inhabitants to recant. The *parfaits* replied simply: 'Why preach at us? We have our own faith and care nothing for the Church of Rome!'

On 22 July 1210 a huge stake was erected in Minerve. This was to be the location of the first of the really great holocausts in which Christians incinerated Christians in the name of Christ. Some 140 *perfecti* – and not one of them had 'fired a shot in anger' – went to the flames on that day. A chronicler wrote: 'Our men were not put to the trouble of throwing them into the fire, so joyfully did they embrace their heresy that they hurled themselves into the flames.'

If you go to Minerve today, you will see adjacent to the church a small memorial stone to these Cathars. At the top of the stone the shape of a dove, the symbol of the Holy Spirit, has been carved out so that you can look right through the stone, and what you see on the other side is framed by the head and wings of this dove.

Vals

Some 35 kilometres southwest of Fanjeaux there is a village called Vals. Its church hugs closely to the ascending slopes of the beautiful valley of l'Hers. Vals is well off the main road between Pamiers and Mirepoix and the traveller today might well never see this place. That would be a sad omission for the church of Vals is a rare sight. It is constructed both within and above a barrow-like rock which was once the site of a prehistoric temple. Carved into the rock is the oldest part of the church, the nave, and it was built in the tenth century. The chancel was added a century later. Then, from out of the rock ascends a rectangular tower like a lighthouse on which a simple enclosure houses a single bell. The tower was constructed in the twelfth century. Entry to the church is made through what appears to be a cave in the side of the rock. There is another chapel on a second level while the third level leads to the tower stairs.

From 1209 to about 1227 we know that the seigneur of Vals, Guillaume Adémar, knight, assisted Cathar preachers in their house at Mirepoix. His sister, Bérangère was a *parfaite*. He received the *Consolamentum* at his death. But when we look above the altar we see something which raises a question in our minds. Painted within the steep curve of the ceiling we can see quite clearly the remains of a series of frescoes probably executed by Catalan artists for Adémar's ancestors in about 1100. They depict scenes from the gospels and include the Annunciation of the Virgin, the Baptism of Christ and the Adoration of the Magi in a richly emblematic rather than 'realistic' manner. In one of the frescoes, Christ is seen giving the 'keys of the kingdom' to St Peter. Since this was one of the chief doctrinal foundations for the claims to primacy of the Church of Rome – for Peter is held to have founded that church, one can see that such a representation would have been anathema to a Cathar. How is it that Guillaume Adémar, knight, could reject the form of piety observed by his ancestors?

Perhaps we can begin to understand the reason if we consider that in the hundred years since the painting of the frescoes, a good deal of money was being made in the towns of the Languedoc, particularly by merchants. The lords, however, depended for their income on the collection of revenues from the people they protected. Furthermore, it was the custom in these parts for land to be divided among all the children of a deceased lord with the inevitable result that takings became smaller and smaller. Meanwhile the church depended on the nobles for patronage. Bearing in mind the inevitable disputes over ownership of parcels of land, some of which were claimed by the Church, this was clearly not a situation destined to reveal the Catholic clergy in their best light as exemplars of spirituality and self-denial. At the same time, Cathars arrived and, in the words of R.I. Moore, they offered 'a high standard of spiritual performance in return for very low material demands or none at all whereas the Catholic clergy are known to have made rather high material demands in return for low spiritual performance'.

If the local seigneur was a Cathar then he could expect his peasants to follow suit. I wonder how many continued to use the splendid church?

The Inquisition

The first Albigensian Crusade petered out in 1217. A brief crusade was led by the king of France, Louis VIII, in 1226. But in 1229 Raymond VI's son, Raymond VII, Count of Toulouse was granted the rights back to large parcels of his former territories – on the condition that he make serious efforts to persecute heretics. There were rather lacklustre efforts to pursue this end but it was not until April 1233 when the Dominican Order of Friar Preachers (Dominic himself had died 12 years earlier) were granted the right to inquisition by the Pope that the business really got going. This was the founding proper of that institution which has abided in popular memory to this day. Languedoc was at the sharp end of their work for about a century. Their method was straightforward. First they arrived in town and declared that if anyone came forward admitting heresy with the desire to recant they could do so without penance. If nobody came forward they continued on. If somebody did come forward, the person was then required to name all those other heretics he or she knew. These people were then called before the Inquisition and questioned. If they recanted they were given penances which ran the gamut from fasting, having to go on pilgrimage (which could be very expensive) to flogging. Probably the most hated form of penance was that of the imposition of two large and distinctive crosses which had to be sown to the outer garments of the ex-heretic. As one might expect, people were afraid of fraternizing with such a person for fear that he might report them to the Inquisition. When before the Inquisition you could not call witnesses and you were not entitled to debate any point. You were there simply to answer questions. If a person went back to heresy or if he or she refused to recant, then that person was delivered to the secular power for burning. A heretic's property became forfeit and it has been said that the Dominican Inquisition became the largest property brokers in the region.

Since the Inquisition could take no money for themselves, it could be advantageous for local authorities and others to help the Inquisition. It would appear that the fundamental attitude of the Inquisition allowed for intensification and development. In the early sixteenth century, Henry Cornelius Agrippa wrote of the Inquisition in his *De vanitate scientiarum* (On the vanity of the sciences):

> But If the person for whom Inquisition is made, do then go about to defend his opinion with testimonies of the Scripture, or with other reasons, they interrupt him with great noise and angry checks. They say that he hath not to do with bachelors [of Arts], scholars in the chair, but with Judges, in the judgement seat, that there he may not strive and dispute, but must answer plainly, if he will stand to the decree of the Church of Rome, and to revoke his opinion, if not, they show him faggots and fire, saying, that with heretickes they may not contend with argument with Scripture, but with faggots and fire.

This is from a chapter called 'On the Inquisitor's art' and in the 300 years since the persecution of the Cathars, that Art had no doubt been perfected. The Inquisition was despised in the Languedoc. Its operators were mostly strangers to the region and had effectively assumed the role of the state police of the Church of Rome. In May 1242, the son of Guillaume Adémar, seigneur of Vals, also called Guillaume, took part in a fateful mission. As companion-in-arms to Pierre-Roger of Mirepoix, he joined a party of knights (not *perfecti*) who descended from the still unmolested fortress of Montségur (about 40 kilometres to the southeast of Vals) to ride to Avignonet, a town between Carcassonne and Toulouse, to execute vengeance upon a party of inquisitors who had arrived there. They cut down four inquisitors and their retainers. The incident has gone down in history as a massacre.

This outrage led to the climax of our tour. A council was held in Béziers in 1243 and it was there decided to take once and for all the last important citadel of Catharism: Montségur.

Montségur

Although not perhaps the most spectacular site connected with the Cathars – the ruined castle of Termes (captured in November 1210) situated on a mountain peak among the dense forests of the Corbières provides perhaps a more romantic setting for the active imagination – Montségur is certainly the most terrifyingly grim and most significant location with which to end our tour.

The mountain, some 1,207 metres high, rises amid the highest of the Ariège. The castle, somewhat restored so that one can at least discern its strange shape – rather like a long tapering shoe-box – stands upon a 'pog' or rocky pillar at the top of the mountain. From the eastern approach it presents a relentless series of forbidding crags which rise up to the castle battlements. On the western side is a steep forested approach at the foot of which clings the village of Montségur.

It has been conjectured that in prehistoric times the site was a temple to the sun, but no evidence for this has been brought forward. However, it is true that there are four apertures in the walls carved in twos and which are aligned to the rising sun of the summer solstice. This has provided food for rich speculations.

The Seige of Montségur (1243–44)

Although Raymond de Péreille rebuilt the castle in about 1204, Montségur did not become the official centre of Catharism until the eve of the inquisitors' operations in 1232 when Guilhabert de Castres asked Raymond de Péreille to further ensure the safety of the château and its growing number of inhabitants. Raymond called upon his cousin, Pierre-Roger of Mirepoix, a professional knight, for assistance. He provided about 100 knights and sergeants for the protection of the now 400 to 500 Cathars living within and about the castle. Between 1232 and 1243

Montségur was the magnet drawing in not only those escaping from the Inquisition but also the knights and their ladies who came to visit and assist the *perfecti*. Scattered about the castle, *parfaits* and *parfaites* lived a life of contemplation and meditation in small enclosures – so perhaps the atmosphere may be said to have resembled a Tibetan monastery for Buddhist monks.

After the council of Bézier's decision to put an end to Montségur, a huge army was assembled under the leadership of the Archbishop of Narbonne and the king's seneschal of Carcassonne, Pierre Amiel. Montségur proved for ten months to be the impregnable fortress it very much appears to be. Inside the castle there were about 205 *perfecti* (of whom it is possible to identify 58 by name), a garrison of about 100 (65 of whom we know by name) and a population of women and children of whom we know the names of 131. They were being supplied by villagers of Montségur who knew the terrain perfectly. The siege appeared vain until just before Christmas 1243 when a party of Gascon climbers gained access to a look-out post on the crest opposite the castle, slit the throats of the defenders and so created a passageway for the troops who were thus able to steadily seize the castle approaches.

The Treasure of Montségur

At this point the now legendary treasure of Montségur was removed from the castle. Some have thought that this treasure included the Holy Grail or the lost treasure of the Jerusalem temple. Such speculations are unnecessary. We know from Inquisition records that Montségur was the Cathars' 'bank'. The treasury included gold, silver and a lot of money which had been donated to the cause of maintaining the 'true' Christianity through the worst of the persecution. The money was needed to support those Cathars in hiding in the forests and grottoes of the Ariège and the Corbières. We know the names of two of the male *perfecti* who removed the treasure. They later turned up in Lombardy (north Italy) where Cathar *émigrés* from the Languedoc fled.

It seems that the legend surrounding the treasure can be accounted for by the confluence of firstly, the simple fact of the treasure's existence and secret removal before the fall of Montségur, secondly, by the symbolic meaning of Catharism itself – as a doctrine which would be to gnostic perception a treasure of the spirit, akin to Christ's symbolism and allegory of the 'pearl of great price' and of the treasure buried or disregarded, and, thirdly, from the act or event of the 'collective imagination', seizing upon the implication of a pure spiritual message amidst an emotionally intense series of violent historical events.

The Tragedy of Montségur

What follows is not the stuff of legend but of fact. Around 21 February 1244, bombardment of the castle by catapult commenced. Massive shells weighing 80 kg are still being discovered in the forests below the castle. This fierce attack was repulsed, but by 2 March 1244, Pierre-Roger of Mirepoix was compelled to sue for a 15-day truce. In that time the *perfecti* distributed their food and clothes and prepared themselves for a 'death' they did not believe in.

On the Sunday before the final capitulation (13 March) something extraordinary happened, which, for the historian Michael Rocquebert, 'represents the true secret of Montségur'. Twenty *crédentes* asked the leading *parfait* Bertrand Marty to be 'consoled'. As ordinary Cathar believers they could survive the capitulation. As *parfaits* and *parfaites* they knew that they would be burned alive.

On 16 March 1244, the castle of Montségur was surrendered to the Archbishop of Narbonne and the seneschal of Carcassonne. On that day, 225 male and female *perfecti* were led to a stake on a plateau below the 'pog' and summarily burned.

Armed resistance to the Catholic armies was at an end. The survivors were interrogated by the Inquisition. Nineteen documents of interrogation have come down to us and from these records comes our principal information for the siege and collapse of Montségur.

Standing on a mountain opposite the pyramidal aspect of Montségur in July 1986, the historian Robert Moore asked Michael Rocquebert what the significance is for us of this terrible event:

> It was certainly a great tragedy brought about by intolerance and I think that if the world today is turning its attention to Catharism and its history with so much curiosity and so much emotion, it is because people see in Montségur the symbol, the sign, of eternal intolerance. There is also in Catharism food for very deep spiritual and religious reflection, of that I am absolutely convinced.

As is the author.

Chapter Six

What happened to the Cathars?

Without doubt, the Albigensian Crusade and the siege of Montségur confirmed the Cathar in his knowledge of what kind of power controlled the world. Nevertheless, the horror of Montségur, the fall of the citadel of the spirit, must have traumatized the *crédentes* if not the surviving *perfecti*. Although the loss of Montségur threw the organization of the Cathar Church into confusion, the Cathars were not finished but persisted clandestinely in forests, mountains, caves and in the more remote villages of the Pyrenees. The Inquisition was still occupied in the area about Pamiers in the early fourteenth century where the Bishop Jacques Fournier's Inquisition would one day furnish Emmanuel Le Roy Ladurie with the source material for his book *Montaillou*. The last Cathar to be burned was a popular inhabitant of Villerouge-Termènes, Bélibaste in 1321. The village honours Bélibaste today in an equally popular festival held in August.

Three major questions remain to be answered.

Were the Cathars a menace to society?

This is highly unlikely. In the first place, it should be noticed that although the great counts of the region supported and tolerated the Cathars - while members of their families did become *perfecti*, there is no evidence that the great powers themselves were *crédentes*.

Inquisition records of 1246, soon after Montségur, reveal very few Cathars – in Fanjeaux 28; in Laurac 30 – and these numbers are exceptional. Elsewhere, no more than handfuls could be detected. Furthermore, there is no evidence to suggest that Catholics and Cathars did any more than peacefully coexist. When at Albi in 1234 the inquisitor Arnaud Cathala authorized the exhumation of dead heretics for post-mortem condemnation and burning, he was roughly handled by a 'mob' enraged at an action repugnant to all. There is an account of how when one knight was asked why he did not pursue the heretics, he replied:

'How could we do that? We have seen them brought up. We have been brought up side by side with them – our closest kinsmen are among their number. Every day we see them living worthy and honourable lives in our midst.'

On another occasion a priest secured a recantation from a Cathar on condition that they play chess for the penance – the priest lost! Lax as this may appear, none the less the priest should have been commended for obtaining a recantation without violence – no common occurrence. In short, there was peaceful coexistence until outsiders moved in.

So why were the Cathars persecuted?

Firstly, the Cathar church did threaten the power and influence of the Church of Rome. That is clear enough. The Church of Rome has never enjoyed competition.

Secondly, the concerted persecution of Cathars offered great opportunities to those unscrupulous men who could muster an army against them. The Counts of Toulouse wanted the counties of Carcassonne and Béziers, the kings of Aragon wanted the county of Toulouse and Simon de Montfort (father, by the way, of the man who compelled England's King John to sign Magna Carta) wanted whatever he could get. It has been said in the latter's defence that he was a deeply religious man. Is that an excuse?

Thirdly, and perhaps most importantly, observers of humanity have often been dismayed at the phenomenon of a special horror and hatred reserved by the powerful for those who renounce the world. A deep consideration of this may lead us to the conclusion that the *bons hommes* – the good men were burned because they were good men. It is significant that one of the things which a suspected Cathar had to deny before the Inquisition was the conviction that the Cathars were good men. Furthermore, their reputations were subjected to further degradation, as their influence declined, by their being called 'buggers' or worse. This was the price to be exacted from those who took Christ seriously when before the judgement-seat of Pilate He said: '*My kingdom is not of this world.*'

Why then did the Cathars disappear?

It may have crossed readers' minds that a religion under persecution is as likely to grow in numbers as it is to decline. Some explanation then is required for the eventual disappearance of authentic Catharism from history.

Firstly, one must consider the effect of the loss of noble support. After 1232 a lord who patronized Cathars was in danger of losing his estate – if he or she had not done so already. Since the peasants tended to follow the creed of the lord, that would account for a significant loss of Cathars. Furthermore, it is unlikely that many ordinary people were fully cognisant of the strict differences between Cathar and Catholic and so would tend to 'go with the tide'. After 1244, the tide was definitely flowing in a Catholic direction.

Secondly, after 1232 and more so after the fall of Montségur, it became extremely hazardous for the *perfecti* to operate and remuster support from a possibly despairing following. Since the *perfecti* were the crux and the heights of the religion, the *crédentes* were doubtless left without guiding examples. A corollary of this situation is that perennial gnostic problem of presenting a religion of perfection. This in itself is not conducive to continuity over a prolonged period. To quote the English historian Bernard Hamilton in *The Albigensian Crusade*: 'It should not be forgotten that they [the *perfecti*] did not succeed in imposing their ethic of non violent other-worldliness on the mass of their believers.' While Professor Hamilton's words are ill-chosen – it was not for the *perfecti* to 'impose' anything; also they were fully aware of Christ's dictum that, 'narrow is the way and few be they that find it' – it is doubtless a significant point if, that is, continuity as a 'church' is seen as having a high value.

Thirdly, new Catholic Orders were put into practice, for example the Franciscan Order and, in the Languedoc region, the 'mendicant friars' adopted many of the habits of the *perfecti* and brought an attainable spirituality within reach of the 'grass roots' while remaining a part of the whole society. Spirituality with security in this world proved to be a winning incentive. The Cathars paid a high price for bringing the best out of the mendicant friars. Catholicism thus started to become a strong force for social cohesion, especially after the *de facto* union of Church and State following the passing of the Languedoc into the control of the French crown in 1271.

Nevertheless, anti-clericalism grew in some parts into a tradition which, denied an organized alternative continues to this day as a contributing factor to a secularized and 'liberal' consciousness.

Fourthly, there developed divergences of opinion within the Cathar tradition, particularly with regard to the nature of the operative dualism, that is, whether reality was sundered by equally opposing principles of good and evil or whether evil represented a rebellion against a primary principle of Good. Sadly, the essential dualism of matter and spirit began to take second place to an impossible metaphysics. Over-commitment to speculation is guaranteed to see the end of any organization no matter how non-hierarchical it may be.

The fifth and last explanation is perhaps not an explanation at all. By virtue of this, it may yet be found to be fundamental. It brings us to a mystery, that mystery which becomes apparent when we ask about a familiar event or place – 'Why here?', 'Why there?' or 'Why at all?'

In short, the success of the Cathar gnosis can be put down to an ingredient in the 'pot' so to speak, which is unknown – something in the 'times'. The Germans, agile at creating new words as ever have given us the much-abused term *zeitgeist* – 'time ghost', 'time spirit', 'spirit of the times'. There is a familiar feeling that occurs to those who have studied the story of the Gnosis when one begins to ponder unknown quantities, undetermined factors, even unseen agencies.

There are discernible eras ('aeons' the gnostic calls them) when there is an awakening of the spirit. It awakes hand in hand with favourable social, political and religious conditions and determinations. In the story of the Cathars we have cited several of them, including warfare and power-struggle set amid a 'liberal' atmosphere and cultural renaissance expressed in the romance and poetry of the troubadours – and then, the tradition subsides for a while into an invisible unconscious mind from which the gnostic impulse derives. '. . . for you are from it and to it you will return' (*The Gospel of Thomas*).

The spiritual energy within man himself must contend with those energies outside his self. If the Gnostic does not withdraw into that shrine, he or she is likely, during inclement conditions, to be overcome by those forces (whether called demiurge, archon or *Rex Mundi*) which make up the fabric of the organism and of the outer spectral world.

The amazing attempt to penetrate the Tragedy of life and so to unify the inner and the outer worlds is the subject of Part Three of this book. It is about those who wished to bring the 'Devil's Creation' into harmony with the spiritual realm of the Absolute Godhead – the next manifestation of the gnostic impulse in our history: the Hermetic philosophy.

The Hermetic Philosophy

Chapter Seven

Hermes comes to Florence

It is perhaps strange that amid the intensity of technological events, people feel a compulsion to employ the language not of reason but of imagination to express themselves. 'That's one small step for man, one giant leap for mankind', is one of the host of fine phrases uttered when greeting the unknown. What if Neil Armstrong had then proceeded to step into a hidden trench and so disappeared from view? Would that have rendered his words vain? Were the words valid anyway? The astronaut spoke as if he had succeeded in uniting the event of stepping onto the lunar surface to the main 'body' of human history. We believed him.

Part Three of this book deals with an analogous attempt to unite the imaginative and the real. The embracing of the Hermetic philosophy by certain men of the fifteenth and sixteenth centuries represents an emboldened leap of creative imagination, from a 'lower' or 'inner' world of non-rational and unconscious strivings, to a principle of Unity which would itself unify human concerns and reorient them towards a new sense of the possible and the real. As we shall see, it began to be seen that the scope of the rational mind, fused in a gnostic manner to the divine mind, was practically infinite. Unlike the Cathar who had felt the earth to be the Devil's creation and a prison, the Hermetic imagination held, it was thought, the keys to Man's eternal freedom. If nothing else I hope that the ensuing chapters show the value, and pitfalls, of the creative imagination – the very 'window', as it were, of gnostic perception – in the human being's unfinished and perhaps tragic struggle for the security of Knowledge.

Florence 1460

The learned men of Florence in the late fifteenth century appear to have moved amid a great sense of nostalgia, a yearning for the past characterized by what we may truthfully describe as wishful thinking, the power to imagine. Any person who has visited Florence cannot help but be amazed or even overcome by the artistic legacy of this period. Florence and Renaissance Art have become almost synonymous terms. From Michelangelo's David to Botticelli's Primavera, from the Duomo to the Church of Santa Maria Novella, from the villas of Fiesoli to the cloisters of San Marco this astonishing city continues to cast a spell upon the visitor. The outpouring of the visual imagination, this we can see in abundance, but the philosophical imagination, if we may use such a term, is not always so visible although there is no doubt that many great works of painting and sculpture have been inspired by it. The beauty of Florence is a testimony to a living world of imagination and it was such a world that provided a welcome new home to the Hermetic philosophy. So when we speak of wishful thinking and of a profound nostalgia we can say that such impulses are likely to precipitate very real effects when close to a given philosophy. The philosophy that was attracting most attention in the Florence of our period was that of Plato. As you may remember, Plato received a similar welcome and development in second-century Alexandra when and where the Hermetists operated, as described in Part One. Fifteenth-century Florentines with a taste for Plato were apt to read him not only in his own works such as the *Timaeus* (which was such an inspiration to Valentinian Gnostics), the *Symposium* and the *Phaedo*, but also in conjunction with the works of neoplatonists who developed or indeed perverted their masters' philosophy. The world of neoPlatonism is that of the hey-day of the Gnosis in the second and third centuries and there is kinship between them. This kinship can particularly be seen in the use of the concept of the 'great chain of being' which sets the world a great distance from the pure realm of divine spirit. Such a view would give justification to a person who felt that this world was somehow 'out of touch' with reality and he himself 'out of touch' with the world. The Platonism of the time then was a rather mixed bag and this doubtless caused a certain amount of confusion, especially for those who were attempting to reconcile the attractions of Platonic philosophy to the rigours of Catholic theology. One of the chief ways to show the divine inspiration of Plato – and therefore his suitability to be described as a 'Theologian' was to point out the correspondence between the Christian Heaven where all things exist in perfection, with God the Father enthroned at its centre and His angels round about Him singing His praises, and Plato's philosophy of a formal and intelligible world where all terrestrial and material things find their perfection, their 'Forms' and their 'Ideas'. In Plato's intelligible world, that is to say the real world, there is neither corruption nor change. This world exists simultaneously with the world of ordinary perceptions – 'our' world. Our world is a kind of shadow of the real and to become aware of this is to become dissatisfied, or, in other words, to become a philosopher, concerned only with the real. This material world is an image derived from or reflecting an eternal idea, thus, for example, *Time* is 'the moving image of *eternity*'. Now it might be deduced from this statement that what binds us to the image of Time and its associated change and decay, is our ignorance of eternity. Here lies a seed for the desire for gnosis as knowledge-of-the-eternal. What if one could penetrate the image and gain knowledge of the eternal? This was the substance of much wishful thinking going on in fifteenth-century Florence. Within the power of the Imagination, the Platonic world can exist and has power to inspire the soul. This principle of correspondence was known to those learned who had encountered magical and alchemical literature. A key alchemical formula known throughout the Middle Ages was that contained within the *Emerald Table* and attributed to none other than Hermes Trismegistos, Thrice-great Hermes who we encountered in Part One. The principle in question is a key to understanding the transforming power of Hermetism: 'It is true and no lie, certain and without deception. What is above is like that which is below, and what is below is like that which is above, to effect a wonderful work.'

The formula can well be adapted to the Platonic theory of the intelligible world, that world which the great neoplatonist philosopher Plotinus (third century) held could only be apprehended by the *nous*, the higher intellect or reason, containing intuitive power – the gnostic faculty *par excellence*. It should be noted here that Plotinus castigated certain Gnostics in Alexandria and Rome precisely for their not employing this faculty.

The result of this reasoning is that as the 'higher' world is like the 'lower' world which we inhabit, so the 'inner' world, enlightened by the penetrating *nous* which can perceive the 'higher' world, has the power to transform the outer world according to the gnosis attained. If not to transform, then certainly enter into. In this act of enlightened entry into the world of sense, and then behind the world of appearances into the intelligible world, we find the harmonious progression of incarnate souls through the world and on to God which fifteenth-century Florentine Platonists held to be the purest account of the Christian life. In the purely Christian understanding of this *type* of redemption, the motive force or force of attraction is Love – Love is moved by Love into Love. This was the theme of a good deal of poetry composed in Florence at this time. But what if the 'motive power', so to speak, became or was seen to be, not the Love of God but the desire for gnosis and its attendant promise of knowledge of things and therefore power over them? This conflict, inherent within the mixed-bag of Renaissance philosophies, was yet invisible but would emerge as time moved on.

Let's return to our theme of wishful thinking. We have seen that there was some awareness of the principle that what is conceived in the mind is as likely to become objectively real as what was once held to come from the will and counsels of God. Slowly, but perceptibly, Man was taking a greater role in the running of the universe. But before we feel too much forboding let us remember that we are still in the honeymoon period of Man's assumption of responsibility – and one of the chief benefactors of that honeymoon was Hermes Trismegistus.

Our mothers tell us we must be careful about what we wish for – it might come true! What was the wish of some of our learned friends in Florence? We may say that the wish of the Renaissance Platonist and unwitting gnostic was for a divinized world, harmonious and true in which Man could resume his place among the celestials and walk – and indeed 'fly' – in freedom towards the still centre of God. The wish was to return to the One, the source from which the power derived enabling the philosopher-magician to work the 'miracle of creation'. Christ had opened the way, the 'veil of the temple' had been rent and the true followers of Christ could ascend. 'Hermes', he of ancient wisdom, mediator between spirit and matter, with winged feet and winged mind was both prophet and symbol of this possibility.

But what would the gnostic imagine he was ascending into? It was the custom among the Platonist philosophers of this time to employ the system of 'Celestial Hierarchies' written, it was thought, by Saint Paul's Athenian convert, Dionysius the Areopagite. It was not the work of this man but of a neoplatonist philosopher of about the fifth century. In its essentials, the Celestial Hierarchies describes three worlds of which ours is the lowest. This is the elemental world of nature and is subject to influences from above. Above this 'sublunary' world, is what is called the 'celestial' world wherein are found the stars and their 'spirits' or 'guardians' (analogous to the Gnostic archons). Even higher is the sphere of the 'supercelestial' world, the world of *nous*, the 'intellectual' or 'intelligible' world of angelic spirits, of superior knowledge of reality because closer to the One, the divine source of creation, who is beyond the three worlds. Hand in hand with this concept of worlds, of which ours is the lowest projection, goes its essential counterpart: the concept of microcosm. It is important to grasp this concept if one is going to have any understanding of what the Hermetist is talking about. The whole system which was seen as going beyond this planet to the distant perfection of the One also exists within the fabric of the human mind. Going deeper and deeper into the mind of Man, illuminated by *nous*, Man could travel farther and farther into the universe – and back again. The possibilities, once one had established correspondence between the inner and the outer worlds, seemed positively infinite – and any new information which would deepen such understanding was eagerly sought.

So we can see that this enthusiasm for the 'return to the One' was a corollary of that desire to revivify the world of Antiquity by obtaining the most ancient sources of wisdom. One returned to the source of things by going back to the times when it was thought our world was young, a world of heroes and of magic, of wise men and faithful women – back to the morning when Adam named the animals, when the lion and the lamb played together. If one could recover more of this world, why, one would be gazing at the dawn of a new age.

This taste for antiquity was fuelled in the late fifteenth century by the arrival of new texts from Greece. Greek was older than Latin, Greek was the language of Plato. What new glories awaited the eager *aficionado*?

In 1460, a certain Brother Leonardo of Pistoia, returning from Macedonia, brought a Greek manuscript to Florence. He came to Florence because it was well known that the ruler of Florence, the old Cosimo de Medici was a serious collector of Greek manuscripts. His buying agents travelled all over the Mediterranean gathering the works of Antiquity. Cosimo had heard in various church councils of the existence in Greek of the complete works of Hermes Trismegistus. At this time, Hermes had a great and mysterious reputation. Saint Augustine himself had written of him:

> as for morality, it stirred not in Egypt until Trismegistus's time, who was indeed long before the sages and philosophers of Greece, but after Abraham, Isaac, Joseph, yea and Moses also; for at the time when Moses was born, was Atlas, brother of Prometheus, a great astronomer, living, and he was grandfather by the mother's side to the elder Mercury, who begat the father of this Trismegistus.
>
> (*Civitas Dei*, XVIII. 29)

The Christian poet Lactantius writing in about AD 400 wrote of Hermes Trismegistus as a veritable prophet of Christ. In his *Institutes* he wrote that 'Trismegistus, who by some means or other searched into almost all truth, often described the excellence and the majesty of the Word.'

This general approval of Hermes by great Christian authorities from the past was tremendously encouraging to those who wished to combine Greek philosophy and the wisdom of the ancients with Christianity into one universal system of knowledge.

Cosimo was delighted by the new manuscript, for it consisted of nothing less than 14 *libelli* attributed to Hermes. Hermes, the fount from which Plato had drunk. Hermes, a near contemporary of Moses, an inspired prophet, a profound philosopher. Hermes had arrived in Florence and Cosimo had 'got him'! The arrival can be compared to the discovery of the Nag Hammadi Library or of the Dead Sea Scrolls – possibly more so because Cosimo and the Platonist circle about him were believers. Indeed, in spite of the near worship of Plato, Cosimo insisted that his court scholar Marsilio Ficino leave aside the complete works of Plato and get straight on with translating what came to be called the *Pymander* of Hermes Trismegistus. *Pymander* was the title given to the Greek *Poimandres*, possibly meaning, 'Shepherd of Men' – the title of the first book of the *Corpus Hermeticum*. Cosimo wanted to read the work before he died. Ficino completed the translation in a few months and Cosimo's wish came true before his death in 1464. Ficino's original translation is now in the Medici Library in Florence. The stunningly beautiful manuscript begins with an introduction by Ficino himself. It is like reading 'Alice in Egypt' so charming is its fairy-tale, child-like understanding of remote Antiquity, now brought to light: 'In that time in which Moses was born flourished Atlas the astrologer, brother of Prometheus the physicist and maternal uncle of the elder Mercury whose nephew was Hermes Trismegistus.'

The *Corpus Hermeticum*, inspirer of Plato the Theologian and of all philosophy, spoke in a pristine simplicity of Man's original nature within the supercelestial realms where he consorted with angels and was privy to the mind of God, indeed was part of that mind. This all chimed in with the nostalgia we have mentioned and its corollary: the yearning for a *prisca theologia*, the original theology, the pure untainted divine wisdom. Ficino writes:

> He is called the first author of theology: he was succeeded by Orpheus, who came second amongst ancient theologians: Aglaophemus, who had been initiated into the sacred teaching of Orpheus, was succeeded in theology by Pythagoras, whose disciple was Philolaus, the teacher of our Divine Plato. Hence there is one *ancient theology* ... taking its origin in Mercurius [Latin form of Hermes] and culminating in the Divine Plato.

This pristine wisdom was being recovered at the same time as theologians in the north of Europe, in the Netherlands and in England were giving much attention to the study of the New Testament in its original Greek. Of course, one can see in all this seeds of conflicts to come. Men were discovering to their delight and dismay that the inherited philosophy and doctrines of the Catholic Church would not always stand comparison with the presumed older and, therefore, 'truer' texts. Renaissance and reform went hand in hand in these matters. Most readers will have some knowledge of the split of Catholic Christendom effected by Luther and the intensification of reforming movements within the Church which hurtled Europe into long and bloody conflicts for some 200 years, and which find some faint echo in today's Ireland. Few, however, are aware of another reformation of thought which continued during the same period, though we might feel compelled to say that the protagonists were not living in quite the same 'world' as one another.

This other philosophical and religious development was partly inspired by the writings attributed to Hermes or Mercurius Trismegistus when 'his' writings were placed as the *fons* for the gathering of neo-platonist philosophy, Pseudo-Dionysius (Celestial Hierarchies), Pythagoras, Zoroaster, Hebrew Cabala and, of course, Plato.

This development was carried on in the studies of scholars and artists and as such contributed to the imaginative world of sixteenth-century Europe rather than initiating a social movement. This may well be because the Hermetic impulse did not seek the kind of power over men's minds and actions through state or institutional control as that which was sought by the protagonists and servants of the Protestant Reformation and Catholic counter-Reformation. The very philosophies embodied in Hermetism did not encourage worldly thought. Nevertheless, and paradoxically, the world would be subtly affected by the 'new' imaginative context of the Hermetic gnosis.

The willing initiate into the ancient theology could now enter the world of Hermes himself:

> Once on a time, when I had begun to think about the things that are, and my thoughts had soared high aloft, while my bodily senses had been put under restraint by sleep – yet not such sleep as that of men weighed down by fullness of food or by bodily weariness – methought there came to me a Being of vast and boundless magnitude, who called me by my name, and said to me, 'What do you wish to see and hear, and to learn and come to know by thought?' 'Who are you?' I said. 'I,' said he, 'am Poimandres, the sovereign mind (*nous*).' 'I wish to learn,' said I, 'the things that are, and understand their nature, and get knowledge [*gnōnai*] of God. These,' I said, 'are the things of which I wish to hear.' He

answered, 'I know what you wish, for indeed I am with you everywhere; keep in mind all that you desire to learn, and I will teach you.'

This is how the reader first enters the *Corpus Hermeticum*.

Chapter Eight

Pico della Mirandola (1463–94) and the Dignity of Man

We have seen then that the *Corpus Hermeticum* was appreciated as an invaluable aid to the task of restoring the original image of Man: Man as mercurial being, moving from one world to another, or, in Hermetic terms, moving through the image of the world to the source of that image, God Himself.

Giovanni Pico, Count of Mirandola was one of the first Renaissance philosophers to seize upon the full range of possibilities inherent in the new body of Greek sources entering Florence and circulating about the 'brains trust' around the court of Cosimo's successor, Lorenzo de Medici, Lorenzo the Magnificent. To these sources he added his vast and perhaps wildly eclectic knowledge of Hebrew Cabala (theosophical and gnostic writings based on the supposition of a hidden meaning within the books of the Old Testament, revealed by inner contemplation and the manipulation of Hebrew letters: the Language of God), his knowledge of Arabic sources on algebra, geometry, astrology, medicine and astronomy. Pico has been dubbed the 'Phoenix of the wits' by virtue of his fantastic erudition on all the subjects of his day. He was a man of great, almost feminine beauty as his portrait reveals in a fresco by Cosimo Roselli still preserved in the Church of San Ambrogio in Florence. He stands piously and dreamily gazing on a celebration of the Mass, his long blond hair and angelic features shining in the sun. He was only 31 when he died. Already at 24 he had composed 900 theses issued as a challenge to every intellectual knight-errant in Europe to come and debate, before a Florentine public on the feast after Epiphany, 1487.

Nine hundred theses – what an age! Should a challenger be short of funds, Pico offered to pay their expenses. It could have been an amazing event with all the great minds of Europe assembled so that Pico could take them on an intellectual journey from the purest Antiquity to the gates of the future and even beyond there.... The debate never happened.

Several of the propositions came before the eyes of Pope Innocent VIII and he smelt heresy. In a Bull dated 4 August 1487, 13 were selected from the bulk of 900 and were pronounced heretical. Pico, undeterred, hastily put together an 'Apology' defending the 13 contested theses with a severe and dry style, a *tour de force* of the old scholastic style of argument. He dedicated the *Apologia* to his patron and friend Lorenzo de Medici, 'a trifling gift indeed, but as far as possible from being a slight token of my loyalty, nay, of my devotion to you'. The obnoxious theses were themselves not Hermetic in origin but there is a confidence present in the assertions that seems to belong to a new world, and, from the Church's point of view, a dangerous world. Proposition number five, for example, must have caused a few raised eyebrows. It declares that no science affords a better assurance of the divinity of Christ than magical and cabalistic science. Pico further declared that what was relevant for the religious man in the nature of Christ's miracles was not the miracles themselves but the manner in which they were done. Pico is struck by St John XIX. 12: 'Verily, verily, I say unto you, He that believeth on me, the works that I do shall he do also; and greater works than these shall he do; because I go to my Father.'

Pico has perhaps wondered why it has taken mankind so long to discover his full capacities, his full dignity. He knows that such knowledge was familiar to Antiquity but somehow seems to have been lost. In spite of the melancholy sight of an ignorant humanity and a Church 'all too human', Pico is ready to pick up the pieces and announce a new dawn. The substance of this new dawn can be found in the Preface to his 900 theses and which, after his death, enjoyed a wide and appreciative circulation as the *Oratio*, commonly known as the *Oration on the Dignity of Man*.

The Dignity of Man

Many of us have heard of this phrase. It has in modern times been associated with another concept, the 'rights of man' as well as with the myth of Prometheus, he who stole the fire of the gods to liberate mankind, the very *type* for a nineteenth-century revolutionary and Byronic romanticism. What Pico had in mind was something far less mundane. The dignity of man consisted in the knowledge of his spiritual origins; his knowledge of the divine; his freedom to determine for himself whether he be brute or god. In the *Oratio* Pico takes a phrase of Hermes Trismegistus from the dialogue with Asclepius (available in a Latin translation and attributed to Apuleius of Madaura, before the arrival of the Greek *Pymander*) as his text for what would, in the sixteenth century, be understood as the Hermetic programme for a project of no less a scope than the regeneration of the world.

Hermetic Man is not the 'worm of sixty winters', the sad, decaying creature dependent upon graces transmitted by the Church but is, to quote Hermes, a 'mortal god'. This is without doubt a gnostic conception of Man, akin to the Valentinian *Anthrōpos*; the Cabalists' *Adam Kadmon*; primal man, as he was before his descent into matter, as he could be if he awakens to his true identity – this is what is known when the Gnostic saviour begs his hearers to know themselves. It will I hope be both exciting and useful to examine Pico's *Oratio* by taking some key extracts and commenting briefly on them – briefly because a comprehensive commentary on the work could fill several more books.

Pico della Mirandola begins his ungiven oration of 500 years ago with the following words:

> I have read in the records of the Arabians, reverend Fathers, that Abdala the Saracen, when questioned as to what on this stage of the world, as it were, could be seen most worthy of wonder, replied: 'There is nothing to be seen more wonderful than man.' In agreement with this opinion is the saying of Hermes Trismegistus: 'O Asclepius man is a great miracle.'

The quotation is from the Latin *Asclepius* – substantially the same work as that of which a large fragment was found in a Coptic version at Nag Hammadi in 1945. There is no doubt in my mind that the Gnostic Gospels and other Christian gnostic literature can be better understood when approached from a Hermetic direction. For, putting the matter simply, while the Hermetic work has no need of a redeemer figure since the revelation is guaranteed only to the elect initiate, by virtue of his own Nous, the Christian Gnostics saw the Christ figure as offering a gnostic redemption to all those who had 'ears to hear' and preserved a complete gnosis to a few. That is to say that in terms of the philosophy of the Nag Hammadi gospels we are not going too far if we think of it as being essentially 'Hermetic' of varying shades with the absence of Hermes and the addition of Christ or rather the 'Living Jesus' of gnostic revelation. What Pico, and Ficino to a lesser degree, wanted to do was to unite the hermetic revelation with that of Christ, Plato, Artistotle, the Cabala, Pseudo-Dionysus, Plotinus and the other Neoplatonists Porphyry, Proclus and Iamblichus. By a neat twist, this kind of compendiousness also seems to have motivated the assemblers of the 'Hermetic' tractates in the first place. We know that the second century

Carpocratian Gnostics (followers of the antinomian Carpocrates) also wished to assemble all the enlightened minds of the past, for we read in Irenaeus (Against Heresies) of them decking the images of Plato, Pythagoras, and Jesus with garlands. This tells us something about the gnostic tendency to attempt an integration of all inspired utterances within grand systems – in the probable hope that there is in all of them some unifying principle which will lead man to the ground of all being. As Yoko Ono sings, 'We're all one'. Of course, by referring to Yoko Ono, I too am adding to the mythology. For Pico, the unifying principle is in the very existence of Man: 'a living dignity of reverence and honour'. Hermes continues in the *Asclepius*:

> Because he takes in the nature of a god as if he were himself a god; he has familiarity with the demon-kind, knowing that he issues from the same origin; he despises this part of his nature which is but human, because he puts his hope in the divinity of the other part. O what a privileged blend makes up the nature of man! He is united to the gods because he has the divinity pertaining to gods; the part of himself which is of the earth he despises in himself; all those other living things which he knows himself to be tied in the virtue of the celestial plan, he binds them by the tie of love. He raises his sights towards heaven. Such therefore is his privileged role as intermediary, loving the beings who are inferior to him and is loved by those above him. He takes the earth as his own, he blends himself with the elements by the speed of thought, by the sharpness of spirit he descends to the depths of the sea. Everything is accessible to him; heaven is not too high for him, for he measures it as if he were in his grasp by his ingenuity. What sight the spirit shows to him, no mist of the air can obscure; the earth is never so dense as to impede his work; the immensity of the sea's depths do not trouble his plunging view. He is at the same time everything as he is everywhere.

Five years after Pico quoted from this passage, it might have already begun to look like prophecy, for in 1492 Columbus would sail west to find the east.

Having announced the guiding text for his oration, Pico continues:

> At last it seems to me I have come to understand why Man is the most fortunate of creatures and consequently worthy of all admiration and what precisely is that rank which is his lot in the universal chain of being – a rank to be envied not only by brutes but even by the stars and by minds beyond this world.

We note here that 'universal chain of being' so familiar to Neoplatonists and so congenial to the Hermetic imagination.

The best of artisans addressed man thus: 'The nature of all other beings is limited and constrained within the bounds of laws prescribed by Us. Thou, constrained by no limits, in accordance with thine own free will, in whose hand we have placed thee, shalt ordain for thyself the limits of thy nature.'

Thou shalt have the power to degenerate into the lower forms of life, which are brutish. Thou shalt have the power, out of thy soul's judgement, to be reborn into the higher forms, which are divine.' Whatever seeds each man cultivates will grow to maturity and bear in him their own fruit. If they be vegetative, he will be like a plant. If of the senses he will become brutish. If rational he will grow into a heavenly being. If intellectual [of the *nous*], he will be an angel and a son of God. And if, happy in the lot of no created thing, he withdraws into the centre of his own unity, his spirit, made one with God, in the solitary darkness of God, who is set above all things, he shall surpass them all ...

Now, perhaps we come to the heart of the matter:

Exalted to the lofty height, we shall measure therefrom all things that are and shall be and have been in indivisible eternity; and, admiring their original beauty, full of divine power we shall no longer be ourselves but shall become He Himself Who made us.

This is a most remarkable, even ecstatic declaration of Man's potential, truly amazing. With this phrase we may say that man – or at least Pico – has 'recovered' his sense of lost worth; has risen above sinfulness to become a co-creator, the primary active agent in a living universe. Not only is it 'all in the mind' but it is *all* in the mind. Man can choose whether or not he commits sins or whether he 'pants after the highest'. Original sin, Pico implies, can be overcome. To a person living in Italy in the fifteenth century this is possibly equivalent to saying that if we choose to be guided by holy ambition, to mount the spheres to the Godhead, then the threat of nuclear annihilation will cease to be. Gone in a second. Man can now stand with his feet on the ground and his head in the stars:

For he who knows himself in himself knows all things, as Zoroaster first wrote. When we are finally lighted in this knowledge, we shall in bliss be addressing the true Apollo on intimate terms ... And, restored to health, Gabriel 'the strength of God', shall abide in us, leading us through the miracles of nature and showing us on every side the merit and the might of God.

Man can now enter into the very fibre of nature for he has come to know and share in that divine nature which is thereby revealed to be both present in nature and 'behind' or 'above' it. As the Jesus of *The Gospel of Thomas* says, 'Rather the kingdom is spread over the earth, but men do not see it.' What a spur this gives to the natural scientist as well as the alchemist who had long thought on these lines. Man is not only a co-operator with God, he is an operator in the Divine Creation. He can, of course, only regain these powers on being 'restored to health'. But Pico makes it clear that this too is within the human grasp.

For those who were wondering how all these things may be accomplished, Pico offers an introduction to method. His first port of call is the science of number, which, Pico admits, 'I have introduced as new, but which is in fact old, and was observed by the first theologians and by the first Platonists, but which in this present era, like many other illustrious things, has perished through the carelessness of posterity, so that hardly any traces of it can be found.' Pico quotes an obscure 'authority' to the effect that 'he knows all things who knows how to count'. Numbers are going to open up the whole universe and, in the process, man is going to know himself and his Creator.

The next method he proposes is *Mageia* or magic, not he stresses, to be confused with that 'which depends entirely on the work and authority of demons, a thing to be abhorred, so help me the God of truth, and a monstrous thing'. This latter he informs us was called *goetia* by the Greeks and has nothing to do with the 'perfect and most high wisdom' of *Mageia*. This magic is going to be of great service in the matter of taking command of the creative process; it is going to give Man power over the inner workings of nature and grant the insight and invisible power to subvert chaotic and destructive powers, and, 'abounding in the loftiest mysteries, embraces the deepest contemplation of the most secret things, and at last the knowledge of all nature'. The magician is to find the essential structure, the principle of a thing, its 'living' idea by a powerful imaginative sympathy with that thing and to transform the behaviour of that thing – so long as the magician also attains further enlightenment of the divine mind, reflected in himself through contemplation of nature. What precisely was involved here it is difficult to say but there is no denying the imaginative force of Pico's programme: 'The *mageia*, in calling forth into the light as if from their hiding places the powers scattered and sown in the world by the loving-kindness of God does not so much work wonders as diligently serve a wonder-working nature.'

Within the magical conception of the universe, there is within all things the essence of a universal power, a living power and not infrequently called 'spirit' in the Stoic sense. That is, spirit is seen as substantial, as the most refined substance surely but substance still. Matter according to the theory cannot enter spirit but spirit can enter matter. Spirit is the medium of Hermes as the winged messenger; the Hermetic magus has something to 'work with'. And what is that work? Pico puts it succinctly: 'As the farmer weds his elms to vines, even so does the magus wed earth to heaven, that is, he weds lower things to the endowments and powers of higher things.'

The magus is to be devoted to the raising of earth (matter) to heaven (spirit). The method, or secret of working lies within the gnosis or knowledge of Man as he is and can be – he knows he has access to the divine world. In a process of contemplation or alchemy he rises through an inner imagination of ascending principles until he feels he is full of 'light'. In such a condition, the *magus* sets to work. That work might be artistic, turning paint into vision, stone into form; mechanical, turning wood and brass into machinery; religious, turning ill thoughts and bitterness into love and brotherhood; landscaping, building, singing, travelling, loving, cooking, writing, capitalizing – the possibilities are endless. In a holy mind the world may be transformed. As 'Jesus' says in the Valentinian *Gospel of Philip*: 'I came to make (the things below) like the things (above, and the things) outside like those (inside, I came to unite) them in that place.' The whole universe awaits transformation and Man, the great miracle, is the one to do the job. 'For the earnest expectation of the creation,' Saint Paul wrote, 'waiteth for the revealing of the sons of God.' 'Wait no more' says Pico, 'We're here!'

If one should ask how it is that men have been formerly ignorant of such dynamic knowledge, Pico gives a clue: 'Think on how Origen the theologian [third century], asserts that Jesus Christ, the Teacher of Life, made many revelations to his disciples, which they were unwilling to write down lest they should become commonplaces to the rabble This is in the highest degree confirmed by Dionysius the Areopagite who says that the occult mysteries were conveyed by the founders of religion, from mind to mind, without writing, through the medium of speech.'

In what could have been a shattering climax to a debate that never was, Pico speaks of the end of the adventure:

We shall fly up with winged feet, like earthly Mercuries, to the embraces of our blessed mother and enjoy that wished-for peace, most holy peace, indivisible bond, of one accord in the friendship through which all rational souls not only shall come into harmony in the one mind which is above all minds, but shall in some ineffable way become altogether one. This is that friendship which the Pythagoreans say is the end of all philosophy. This is that peace which God creates in his heavens, which the angels descending to earth proclaimed to men of good will, that through it men might ascend to heaven and become angels. Let us wish this peace for our friends, for our century.

That was written almost precisely 500 years ago – and we are still trying. Perhaps it is as Hermes asserts to Tat in *Libellus XIII* of the *Corpus Hermeticum* – that we need new eyes:

HERMES: Even so it is my son, when a man is born again; it is no longer a body of three dimensions that he perceives but the incorporeal.

TAT: Father, now that I see in mind [*nous*], I see myself to be the All. I am in heaven and in earth, in water and in air; I am in beasts and plants; I am a babe in the womb, and one that is not yet conceived, and one that has been born; I am present everywhere.

HERMES: Now, my son, you know what the rebirth is.

Do we?

Chapter Nine

An eternal God clothed in an infinite Nature

Man as magus is the end of Renaissance philosophy, the true glory of the age, perhaps its greatest discovery. But the tempests of the following century would dull the glow surrounding the hermetic concept and force its adherents into melancholy or into the shadows. Some of those who espoused the philosophy would be prey to ridicule in their own time and condemnation after their deaths. Henry Cornelius Agrippa of Nettesheim (1486–1535) whom we have had cause to quote in previous chapters was branded as a black magician who skulked about Germany accompanied by a 'familiar spirit' in the form of a dog. He was, in fact, a counsellor to Charles V, Emperor of Germany and was a judge of the Prerogative court. It was this experience which gave him an insight into the affairs of the Dominican Inquisition which he recounts in his *On the vanity of the arts and sciences*. This latter work denies the value of all the sciences and arts of his time, including the magic with which his name has been most associated. All that matters he says, is the knowledge of Jesus Christ – and in this we can hear the voice of the Protestant reform movement of which he seems to have approved. Although the conclusion of the *de vanitate scientiarum* appears to be positively evangelical, there is yet a twist. It speaks of the kind of intense disorder of thought which underlay the meeting of renaissance 'Man the Magus' philosophy and the reforming zeal of the 'new' Christian – happily facing Judgment Day in the belief that his simple untarnished, unexplainable, unsophisticated faith will preserve him. I think the conclusion is worth quoting in full because it signifies most clearly a clash of mentalities which persists to this day – for it is certain that some readers will consider this book to be a vanity:

> Whither then run you headlong, which seek knowledge of them, which have spent all their lifetime in searching it, and have lost time and labour, and could not find any truth? O ye fools and wicked ones, which setting

apart the gifts of the Holy Ghost, endeavour to learn those things of faithless Philosophers, and matters of errors, which ye ought to receive of God, and the Holy Ghost. Will you believe that we can get knowledge out of the ignorance of Socrates? Light out of the darkness of Anaxagoras? Virtue out of the pit of Democritus? Prudence out of the madness of Empedocles? Piety out of the tune of Diogenes, sense out of the peevishness of Carneades and Archesilaus, wisdom out of wicked Aristotle and faithless Averroes? Belief out of the superstition of the Platonics? You err very much, and be deceived by these which have been deceived. But descend into your selves you which are desirous of the truth, depart from the clouds of man's traditions, and cleave to the true light: behold a voice of Heaven, a voice that teacheth from above, and showeth you more clearly than the Sun, why are you your own enemies, and prolong time to receive wisdom; hear the oracle of Baruch: God is as he was and no other shall be esteemed with him, he hath found out all manner of learning, and hath given to Jacob his child, and Israel his beloved, giving Laws and commandments, and ordaining sacrifices: after this he was seen on the earth, and was conversant with men, that is to say, taking flesh, and with an open mouth teaching those things, which under dark questions he hath taught in the Law and the Prophets. And to the end that you may not think, that these things be referred to divine things only, and not to natural, hear what the wise man witnesseth of himself: It is he that hath given me the true knowledge of those things which are, that I might know the dispositions of the compass of the earth, the virtue of the Elements, the beginning, consummation, middle, and revolutions of times, the course of the year, the dispositions of the Stars, the natures of living Creatures, the anger of beasts, the force of the winds, the thoughts of men, the differences of plants, the virtues of roots, and finally I have learned all the things which be hidden and unknown, for the Artificer of all things hath taught me wisdom. The Divine wisdom never faileth, nothing escapeth it, nothing augmenteth it, but comprehendeth all things. Understand you therefore now, that there needeth not much labour in this place, but Faith and Prayer: not the study of long time, but humbleness of spirit and cleanness of heart: not the sumptuous furniture of many books, but a pure understanding, and made fit for the truth as the key is for the lock: for the great number of books chargeth the learner, instructeth him not, and he that followeth many authors erreth with many. All things are contained and taught in the only volume of the Holy Bible, but under this condition – they be not perceived but by them which are made clear: to others they be parables, and dark made fast with many seals. Pray then to the Lord God in faith doubting nothing, that the Lamb of the tribe of Juda may come, and open to you the sealed book, which Lamb alone is holy and true, which alone hath the key of knowledge and discretion, which openeth and no man shutteth, which shutteth and no man can open. This is Jesus Christ, the word and son of God the father and blessed wisdom, the true Master made man as we are, that he might make us the children of God as he is, which is blessed forever. But lest that through using more words I should declaim as it is said, beyond the hour, let this be the end of our Oration.

There is no denying the wisdom of this conclusion. It is especially wise because a few years later, in 1533, Agrippa published his Three Books *de occulta philosophia* – of occult philosophy. 'Occult' here simply means what is hidden; for example, in Agrippa's day, sub-atomic physics or genetic engineering would have been seen as occult practices. It is fairly safe to say that the *Vanity of the Sciences* was published as a kind of 'Apology' for the sins of youth, with the added bonus of serving as a defence for the soundness of his Christian faith should he be, as indeed he was, accused of being a sorcerer. On the other hand, the Vanity also represents a minimalist compendium of knowledge according to the *via negativa* – that approach to religious awareness which starts by affirming what God is not – God is undefinable, the world cannot be known to the degree of certainty. It is a thoroughly sceptical attitude – not a bad attitude for a magician – brought upon all things but the 'word and son of God' who shows knowledge only to those who have not expected to find it in any other place but with the 'true master'. The approach of the Occult Philosophy, on the other hand, is considerably more direct – positive knowledge of God's creation and the manipulation of that power is the programme of the three books. They take us from the natural magic of this world through to the celestial world of Book II and on to the supercelestial world of angelic intellect, the home of *nous*. It is in the celestial world that we find Agrippa coming to terms with man, Hermetic Man, in the chapter entitled, 'Of man, how he was created after the Image of God' we meet the Thrice great Hermes once more:

> The most abundant god (as Trismegistus saith) hath framed two Images like himself, viz. the world and man, that in one of these he might sport himself with certain wonderful operations: but in the other, that he might enjoy his delights, who seeing he is one, hath created the world one ...

Trismegistus was a safe authority at this time because he was held in esteem by ancient Christian authorities. He is even seen as one who had glimpsed the Holy Trinity of orthodoxy. Thus, Agrippa is able to say that 'especially he (Man) shall know God, according to whose image he was made'. The same justification is given for putting the Trinity not above man but within him:

Also Mercurius Trismegistus confessing the divine Trinity, describeth it as understanding, life and brightness, which elsewhere he calleth the word, the mind and the spirit, and saith that man made after the image of God, doth represent the same Trinity; for there is in him an understanding mind, a verifying word, and a spirit, as it were a Divine brightness diffusing itself on every side, replenishing all things, moving and knitting them together: but this is not to be understood of the natural spirit [the *materia prima* of the Hermetic vision] which is the medium by which the soul is united with the flesh and the body, by which the body liveth and acteth, and one member worketh on another.... But we here speak of the natural spirit, which yet in some sort is also corporeal, notwithstanding it hath not a gross body, tangible and visible, but a most subtle body and easy to be united with the mind viz. that superior and Divine one which is in us; neither let any one wonder, if we say that the rational soul is that spirit, and a corporeal thing.

The above translation was made by an unknown translator 'J.F.' in London in 1651 at the height of Oliver Cromwell's government. It testifies to the persistence of the Hermetic philosophy and legend. I say persistence because in 1614 the brilliant scholar of Greek, Isaac Casaubon had shown in his *de rebus sacris et ecclesiasticis exercitiones XVI* that the *Corpus Hermeticum* could not possibly have been written by an ancient Egyptian sage – be he Hermes Trismegistus or anyone else. The Greek style was of the period of Plotinus (second and third century) and, furthermore, it had clearly escaped the attention of former commentators that neither Plato nor Moses nor Aristotle nor indeed any pre-Christian writer had ever made reference to this Hermes Trismegistus. Nevertheless, this new information was largely ignored by committed Hermetists and continued in a more muted form as an underground fantasy of determined occultists well into the eighteenth century, and even beyond.

At almost precisely the same time as Casaubon was quietly demolishing the myth of Hermes Trismegistus, William Shakespeare was composing one of his last great plays, namely, *The Tempest*. There can be no doubt that the character of the magician Prospero is a dramatic presentation of the Hermetic magus; controlling nature, destiny, spirits of sea and air and, finally, bringing the starry plot to a harmonious dénouement in an enchanted atmosphere of love and magic. Shakespeare is clearly on the side of Prospero – as we ourselves feel to be also. Shakespeare would not be Shakespeare if he had been unable to grasp the imaginative nature and power of the Hermetic vision. The way to overcoming religious and racial differences lay all about us; within nature around us; within the rasor-magic of the stars above us, and within the mind of God manifested everywhere: '... the beautiful world of God, the incomparable work, the energy that possesses goodness, the many-formed vision, the abundance that does not envy, that is full of every vision', as the *Asklepios* of the Nag Hammadi Library puts it so very well. This is the vision of the world that permits a Prospero to enter and do his work of transformation and reconciliation:

> Ye elves of hills, brooks, standing lakes, and groves
> And ye that on the sands with printless foot
> Do chase the ebbing Neptune, and do fly him
> When he comes back; you demi-puppets that
> By moonshine do the green, sour ringlets make,
> Whereof the ewe not bites; and you whose pastime
> Is to make midnight mushrumps, that rejoice
> To hear the solemn curfew, by whose aid –
> Weak masters though ye be – I have bedimmed
> The noontide sun, called forth the mutinous winds,
> And 'twixt the green sea and the azured vault
> Set roaring war; to the dread rattling thunder
> Have I given fire, and rifted Jove's stout oak
> With his own bolt; the strong based promontory
> Have I made shake, and by the spurs plucked up
> The pine and cedar; graves at my command
> Have waked their sleepers, oped, and let 'em forth
> By my so potent art.
>
> (*The Tempest*. Act IV. 33–50)

But the tide had turned against this dimension of Renaissance philosophy and experience. The English, or rather, Welsh scholar-magician-astrologer-mathematician-mechanician antiquarian-cartographer sometime diplomat and above all, magus, Dr John Dee, on whom the character of Prospero has been thought to have been based, had died in great poverty at Mortlake in 1608. Although favoured by Queen Elizabeth I and her more advanced courtiers the circle about the profound personage of Sir Philip Sydney – Dee was cast aside by James I. Various 'new brooms' were sweeping across Europe in a frenzy of Catholic counter-Reformation and Protestant (and Catholic) 'witch-hunting'. James I, proud author of the book *Demonologie*, a believer in the reality of active demons was certainly not going to give any assistance or ear to a man who was known to have attempted to make contact with the angels of the supercelestial sphere in the vain search for profound knowledge and enlightenment. The fear of vision was at hand.

Chapter Ten

One symbol, many worlds

We have seen how the sixteenth-century magus sought knowledge (*scientia*) through gnosis, or rather the philosophy upon which such an undertaking might rest. The brilliant work of Dame Frances Yates (d. 1981) has led some historians to think that the impetus gained therefrom contributed to or was instrumental in the development of modern science, because it encouraged certain inquisitive minds to explore nature with the promise of not only enlightenment but power. It is difficult to see, however, that Hermetism gave much direction in the way of scientific method. However, in the sixteenth-century sciences there was not that distinction which we employ today between imagination and objective rationality, that is, the material structure of things. The magus wished to enter into the 'spirit' or Idea of a natural thing. He had to penetrate the appearance of nature through imaginative sympathy. He was not so concerned with isolating rational structure as he was with integrating man and nature, angels and intelligence into a single harmonious whole he could command. I think that the magus was 'turned on' by the imaginative and visionary sense of his work, we might say the romance of his task, the broad sweep of matter and spirit caught up in a moving and divine body. We can see this confusion of divine idea and material structure in Dee's most Hermetic work, the *Monas Hieroglyphica*, (One Hieroglyph), published in Antwerp in 1564. Dee believed he had found a 'hieroglyph', a hitherto hidden 'symbol' which contained in its form the very unifying principle of reality. It is a kind of micro-chip which contains within it all the most elementary principles of the universe. It is to be contemplated upon and fixed in memory as an archetype applicable to all studies. But what is it? If one can imagine a great ocean of *prima materia* which we may call in this context 'spirit', a pure unformed, undirected, unmoving, unmoved homogenous world, then we see the beginnings of the universe. If a hand were to, as it were, drop the *Monas Hieroglyphica* into that ocean of potentials, the *materia prima* would immediately start forming itself into the universe we imagine we know. Dee had found, he believed, the structure of structures and the idea of ideas. In *Theorem XVIII*, John Dee writes:

> Before we raise our eyes to heaven, kabbalistically illuminated by the contemplation of these mysteries, we should perceive very exactly the constitution of our Monad as it is shown to us not only in the LIGHT but also in life and nature, for it discloses explicitly, by its inner movement, the most secret mysteries of this physical analysis.

There we have it, the 'best of both worlds' – secret mysteries *and* physical analysis.

'He who devotes himself sincerely to these mysteries will see clearly that nothing is able to exist without the virtue of our hieroglyphic Monad.' Monad. The One – Dee had found the principle of the universe. He had, he believed, fulfilled the promise of the neoplatonist-gnostic challenge. He had returned to the One! This is what it had all been about, the Dignity of Man, the Divinity of the world. In Dee's copy of Ficino's translation of the *Corpus Hermeticum*, he is shown to have made but few annotations on the text. Perhaps he felt there was nothing to add. But of the few notes he has made, there appears with particular force the phrase: *mundus imago dei* – the world is the image of God. Dee is convinced that he has penetrated the image of the world and found its essential unity, the Platonic Idea of the world. What more could the divinely enlightened mind achieve in cooperation with God now that the Monad had been revealed? In *Theorem XX*, Dee is ecstatic:

> O Omnipotent Divine Majesty, how we mortals are constrained to confess what great Wisdom and what ineffable mysteries reside in the Law which thou hast made! Through all these points and these letters the most sublime secrets, and terrestrial arcane mysteries, as well as the multiple revelations of this unique point, now placed in the Light and examined by me, can be faithfully demonstrated and explained.

If one inverts the great Hermetic phrase, 'the world is the image of God', one approaches the two possibilities. Firstly, the 'pantheism' of eighteenth-century German idealist philosophy and romantic poetry and expressed as, 'God is the image of the world'; and secondly, a more familiar gnostic concept, namely, that 'God is the *image* of the world'. That is, we form a God from our own image. For the Gnostic this is the great error and deception. A Valentinian Gnostic writes about this error in *The Gospel of Philip*, found at Nag Hammadi: 'Men make gods and worship their creation. It would be better for the gods to worship human beings.' For the classic Gnostic, seeking God in the image of the world is likely only to result in the forming or discovery of a demiurge, a false God. Some kind of intuition of this makes the sixteenth-century magus anxious about what kinds of Powers he is dealing with – hence the need to penetrate the 'elemental' sphere to achieve enlightenment from the supercelestial. It is also intuited by those who sought to identify Hermetic philosophy with black magic and necromancy. Meric Casaubon, son of the debunker of the Trismegistus legend, released Dee's spiritual diaries in 1659 to support his belief in the existence of demons. Dee's invoked 'angels' were less than they might seem, Casaubon argues. Indeed, they were. They came from the conflation of old magical texts and Anglican liturgy within the diseased mind of Dee's scurrilous scryer, Edward Kelley.

But I think there is a more serious side to this issue. The Hermetist puts out as it were, an historical warning to those who are trying to attain mastery over nature. It is particularly apposite in our age. The magus warns the inquirer into nature not to be obsessed with structure but indeed to penetrate this world to a more spiritual gnosis which will give form and understanding to the work. The eternal *forms* are 'reflected' but do not exist in the elemental world. That is, a magus would be disturbed at the modern scientific dependence on law and *form*ulae. The more you go into matter in search of the forms, seeing the *ideas* as elemental structures, the more materialistic do your conceptions become. The terrifying result of this is that the human agent will come to operate as a demiurgical or archontic figure, an 'archon', blindly dedicated to power over matter. Surely this intuition is familiar to us in the concept of the 'Mad Scientist' and its accompanying fear of science, which nineteenth-century positivists put down to superstition, offering the example of John Dee as a ridiculous representative of that superstition, so fervently did Dee pray before commencing any Hermetic task.

Plotinus and the whole Platonist tradition has asserted that matter is infinite because it is unbounded by 'form'. Against the Aristotelian concept which puts the eternal forms 'within' the world, as it were, the Platonist does not permit this. Intelligibility and matter cannot exist in the same 'space'. Following this line to its possible conclusion, the scientist who believes he or she is arriving at 'reality' on discovering law, proportion and formula in the material world, is simply mistaken, indeed, he has become bound to those laws – his or her life is now determined and freedom has been lost. Sub-atomic physics since Heisenberg's assertion of the 'uncertainty principle' seems to be approaching something like an understanding of this ancient concept – you do not 'get to the bottom' of Matter. Physicists can look forward to a possibly infinite future of formulizing the phenomena of nature with perhaps little creative result. This is how an 'up-to-date' Hermetist might see the matter of matter.

Giordano Bruno (1548–1600)

This concept of the never-ending series or projecting of relatively valid formulae, expressed as mathematical or geometrical configurations can be seen as having a descendent in the cosmological theories of Giordano Bruno of Nola by Vesuvius in Italy. In particular, in his extraordinary concept of the Infinite Universe. Bruno was an out and out Hermetist, his concepts were primarily religious and not, as we think of the word, analytical. For 'the Nolan' as he liked to call himself, the mind of God expresses itself in the cosmos and can be approached through mathematical and geometrical diagrams. I should say continually expressed because Bruno's universe is a living universe. It is also an infinite universe, for several reasons. Firstly, what eternity is to God, infinitude is to matter. Infinity is the only possible expression of eternity – that is, *being* which is absolutely unconditioned by time. Furthermore, matter cannot be bound because it is not form – the forms, the ideas which are the source of material shapes exist in the intelligible world. As Dorothea Singer puts it in her excellent book on Bruno:

> The infinite universe of Bruno's conception was inevitably regarded by him as what we may call a synthesis of infinite relativity. All things and all thoughts and all individual souls have for him their individual and absolute value, yet each can be appraised only in relationship to the others, and the absolute value of each is merged in its relationship to the infinite whole.

Bruno wrote in *De la causa, principio et uno*: 'These philosophers (Pythagoras and Solomon) discovered their friend Wisdom when they discovered this Unity. For Wisdom, Truth and Unity are one and the same.' God is the essence by which everything has its being. Access to this knowledge is still seen in gnostic terms: 'He who has found this Unity has discovered the indispensable key for the true contemplation of Nature.... Thus you will understand that all is in all but all is not totally and in every mode within each other.'

The primal being *is* the unity and the unity *is* the universe. That does not mean that every thing is God but that they are relative appearances within as it were, the Divine Being: 'Thus everything which maketh diversity of kinds, species, differences, properties, everything which dependeth on generation, corruption, alteration and change is not being or existence but is a condition and circumstance of being or existence which is one, infinite, immobile, subject, matter, life, soul, truth and good.' Bruno's vision of an infinite universe pervaded by an eternal spirit is truly astonishing.

Giordano Bruno was one of the first scholars to publicly defend and promulgate the 'new' universe of Copernicus and he was for a long time considered to be a 'martyr for modern science' chiefly on the strength of this. What interested Bruno about the concept was not so much its being scientifically true, as its being symbolically and religiously true. Copernicus in his work on the *Revolutions of the Celestial Orbs*, published in 1543 had laid waste the Ptolemaic conception of the universe which put the earth at its centre. Copernicus puts the sun at the centre of our solar system. The proposition was declared to be anathema by the Catholic Church. On the printed page of the first edition of this book, beneath a drawing of the new system, Copernicus deliberately quotes Hermes Trismegistus who has declared that the 'sun is the visible God'. This conception of God in his dynamic unity shedding light to life, being expressed in a relatively stable and living object fascinated Bruno and the solar symbolism derived from it was to be the symbol of cosmic unity in Hermetic science and art for a long time. Bruno believed that the sun symbolized the living principle which animates the universe, and that a mysticism or rather gnosticism built around this image would give mankind enormous powers: 'If the corporeal quality perceptible to our sense is endowed with infinite active power, then what will be the absolute totality of active and passive power inherent in the totality of things?' So Bruno wrote in his book *On the Infinite Universe and worlds*.

Such a gnosis Bruno believes to have existed in Ancient Egyptian times – and that its progenitor was Hermes Trismegistus. He takes the Lament in the *Asclepius* for a world, or rather Egypt, which had been raped of its temples, barbarized and ridiculed for its belief in the 'many-formed vision of God' as being, not a prophecy of Christianity, as Christian Hermetists understood it, but as a genuine lament for a lost culture of perfect knowledge and purity which, he, Giordano Bruno is going to bring back. Hermetic-Egyptianism, the 'religion of the world' was the message that Bruno would take with him around Europe as he continued undeterred by fairly predictable responses. His deepest wounds seems to have been inflicted upon himself when he considered how he had been greeted with sarcastic derision by the 'grammarians and pedants', as he calls them, of Oxford University in 1584.

Perhaps he would not have found much difference today. Bruno's gnostic experience was simply too big for most bounded scholars of the time to contain. Bruno's animated, infinite universe did not only put the sun in the centre of our solar system, it also, having removed the centrality of our planet, posited the existence of innumerable worlds, countless suns and solar systems. He approached a concept of relativity with boldness. The apparent movement of the planets and stellar bodies is, he asserts, an illusion brought on by sense perception, that is, we see from 'here' and we think we are looking at 'there' in a fixed relationship – but, in fact, we are also in motion and so a fixed law of universal movement is, for Bruno, impossible to establish absolutely from a fixed point. It is a living universe. Relations of distance are relative; time is an image of eternity, not an absolute within the context of the infinite universe.

Bruno has, as it were, taken the gnostic dualism – matter and spirit, God and the world, light and darkness and exploded it into a new world, imperceptible to sense. Contemplating the infinite One which lies behind all phenomena, we recognize according to Bruno that:

> even in the two extremes of the scale of nature, we contemplate two principles which are one; two beings which are one; two contraries which are harmonious and the same. Therefore Light is depth, the abyss is light unvisited, darkness is brilliant, the large is small, the confused is distinct, dispute is friendship, the divided is united, the atom is immensity.... Here are the signs and proofs whereby we see that contraries do truly concur; they are from a single origin and are in truth and substance one. This, having been seen mathematically is accepted physically.... Here as in a seed are contained and enfolded the manifold conclusions of natural science; here is the mosaic, the disposition and order of the speculative sciences.

The universe is not really a tragic place. It only appears to be because we cannot see the whole movement. 'It is well,' Bruno insists, that this world exists – therefore also that an infinity of other worlds exists – only an infinite universe can comprehend all perfection. All things eventually appear in their proper place:

> Thus on our earth the particle of fire seeking to escape and mount toward the sun, carry ever with them some particles of earth and of water with which they are conjoined; and these becoming increased do thus by their own natural impulse return to their own place.

All things are moving and changing, all things proceed and return, all is relative in the divine and infinite universe. All sorrow is of the moment, all principles which can unite will unite. Every invisible point or centre of the universe is an infinite Pleroma – like a fragment of an holographic image – projecting and receiving being, an infinite number of points of plenitude 'rising from the lowest grade of nature to the supreme highest thereof, from the physical universe known to philosophers to the height of the archetype in whom all theologians believe ... until we reach an original and universal substance, identical throughout the whole, which is Being, the foundation of all kinds and all forms.'

A scientific formula can only ever be an approximation to eternal form. What matters for Bruno, however, it not the 'analysis' or breaking up of the universe by approximate abstraction but the intuition and experience of the One: gnosis in fact.

Rationalist science would go on to approach the universe as if the formulae and laws of matter were identifiable with intelligibility – in Einstein's terms, towards a 'unified field theory' which would give mankind an absolute Knowledge of natural law. When Einstein said, 'God does not play dice', the Gnostic replies, 'You can never know! And if He does, why not play dice with Him?' From the Hermetic point of view, 'knowledge' if gained by analysis of matter only, can only ever be a 'copy' or approximation to the Whole – it is in pure gnostic terms, the limited knowledge of the demiurge, to seize this knowledge as knowledge of the 'All' is fatal – man will find himself living under the tyranny of his own abstractions.

The doctrine that every living thing is the centre of the universe can never be truly acceptable to orthodox Christian doctrine because, essentially that doctrine holds that since the world is fallen, the world is sick and mankind is too ill to be able to find God by his own effort. The Gnostic responds by saying that a leap of consciousness will overcome the sense of conflict in the universe. Christ is truly the healer – how can He be a healer if no one and nothing is healed? The orthodox replies that the universe has not reached that stage yet – we do not yet see the new heaven and the new earth. The Gnostic says, 'I have seen this world and to it I belong.' The orthodox says, 'Then You are outside of the Church for *we* are a Church of sinners.' 'None is righteous. No not one', as the psalm says – if you think you have overcome human nature which is by definition sinful, you are deluding yourself. No amount of knowledge or even gnosis can save us from our nature. The Gnostic damns himself by his own presumptions.'

Giordano Bruno was burned alive as an 'impenitent heretic' in Rome in 1600.

The Everlasting Gospel

Chapter Eleven

From muddy waters to the River of Life

Bruno has taken us about as far as possible as a gnostic cosmologian can. That is to say that in terms of the development of gnostic philosophical cosmology there is no further to go. Let the world catch up with Bruno first! Furthermore, Bruno represents the high point of the Hermetic gnosis as a contribution to mainstream history. Surely, the insights of the Hermetists are not forgotten. A 'golden string' carries the lustre of gnosis onwards to our own time. Nevertheless, after the burning of Bruno in 1600, gnosis goes further and further underground. Shakespeare's Prospero is a kind of last apology for the Hermetic magus before he descends into the shadows. We can see echoes and intimations of gnostic philosophy being put to political purposes among the 'Invisible College' of 'Rosicrucians' in seventeenth century Germany but they do no more than repeat in mythological and alchemical terms what had already been thoroughly developed in the fifteenth and sixteenth centuries. The development of freemasonry in the seventeenth and eighteenth centuries also exhibits syncretistic features of Hermetic thought with its desire to establish temples or 'lodges' as centres of gnostic initiation into a 'brotherhood of light'. It is not clear exactly what kind of light emanates from contemporary Freemasonry but I understand that masons are definitely human, so there are grounds for hope as well as despair. Boys will be boys.

Strands of gnostic thought set in a framework of Jewish Kabbalah, have also contributed to the development of occultism in the nineteenth and twentieth centuries, the high points of which are probably the organization of the Hermetic Order of the Golden Dawn in the 1890s with its occult offshoots such as the Order of the Silver Star founded by the Nietzschean and Tantric mage Aleister Crowley (1875–1947) whose books are now widely read by those seeking an alternative philosophy to prevalent rationalist materialism and institutionalized religion. Crowley declared that we are now living in the 'Aeon of Horus', an age characterized by the behaviour of children in both the creative and destructive sense – and he may well be right. In an imagined situation of 'total' moral, religious and political breakdown, Crowley's creed urges us to find our 'true wills', our 'real selves' and to act in accordance with that unique energy. We have, according to Crowley, no right but to do our wills 'and no other shall say nay'. Conflicting wills are apparently out of the question since we are 'stars' and stars apparently follow their proper course. But will the Era of 'Force and Fire' go on indefinitely? Don't worry hints Crowley, the 'ethic' of 'Do what thou wilt' is only a 'holding ethic' until the next 'aeon' when something like balance and harmony shall reign. Naturally, acts of self-sacrifice are in general regarded with horror as being only a kind of suicide and Christ's death on the Cross is consequently abhorred – as is the 'Virgin's womb', for Crowley promises sex in abundance. How far away we have come from the dignity of Hermes and of Man.

Crowley is, of course, despised by other occultists trying to hang on to the harmonies which were so important to sixteenth-century Hermetists. In such a 'harmonizing' vein we find the elements of 'Theosophy' developed by Madame Helena Blavatsky and promoted in India and England by Annie Besant. It has attempted a fusion of western occult traditions with Hinduism and Buddhism into a rather tawdry universal gnosis which aims to encompass all religion and philosophy. The 'Gnostic Christ' of Nag Hammadi is particularly interesting to such people for 'the Christ' is seen as an example of advanced 'consciousness', and we, advanced humanity, moving in a drama of the evolution of consciousness, can attain 'Christhood' in the same sense as Buddhists talk of 'Buddhahood'. The late Krishnamurti, a popular contemporary writer on awareness wisely chose to remove himself from the attentions of those who saw in him a 'type' of the new man. Every year it seems we have new declarations to the effect that the divine man or 'avatar' from the One has appeared. In 1970 John Lennon felt it necessary to sing 'I don't believe in Beatles' in his wonderful song 'GOD' because of the myth which surrounded them. LSD-bearing, neo-gnostic Timothy Leary had written: 'The Beatles are Divine Messiahs. The wisest, holiest, most effective avatars (Divine Incarnate, God Agents) that the human race has yet produced ... I declare that John Lennon, George Harrison, Paul McCartney and Ringo Starr are mutants. Prototypes of a new race of laughing freemen. Evolutionary agents sent by God, endowed with a mysterious power to create a new human species.' All tongue in cheek no doubt.

While John Lennon and Yoko Ono have shown pronounced gnostic interests, they always stressed the 'humanitarian' commitments and sense of shared humanity which has made them so endearing and inspirational. In a chapter entitled 'The Mysterious Smell of Roses' in his surrealist collection, *Skywriting by Word of Mouth*, published in 1986, John Lennon wrote: 'It seems to me that the only true Christians were (are?) the Gnostics, who believe in self-knowledge, i.e., becoming Christ themselves, reaching the Christ within.' It would seem today that anyone who has not succumbed to rationalist and materialistic thought, and sufficiently blessed with talent is likely to have fastened upon him or her the attributes of guru, magus or divine. Some persons have not been slow to capitalize on this phenomenon. Thought on religious subjects persists amid an appalling lack of clarity, mythology and hokum. When Lennon, for example sang that 'The Dream is Over', he strongly implied the corollary of this statement. 'Wake Up!' Don't believe in false gods. 'Beware of the deep sleep,' says the Jesus of the Gnostic Gospels – yet it would seem that many have awakened only to another dream, the craving for *knowing* being so strong. 'The Unknown is what it is,' said John Lennon shortly before he entered it in 1980. In 'No. 9 Dream' he had sung, 'I believe – yes I believe, More I cannot say. What more can I say?' While the 'gnostic story' of the youth movement of the 1960s and 1970s remains to be written, though *Our Savage God* by R. C. Zaehner might not be a bad starting place for such a study, there are many books now available on the occult developments. Sadly, these developments share the tendency to claim infinity within finitude, or access to universal Truth within fixed orders. The orders themselves are certainly not free from rigid, élitist hierarchical systems or internecine bickering – as a study of the establishment of nineteenth- and twentieth-century 'Rosicrucianism' in America bears out in its panting pettiness.

To this student at least, neognosticism in its innumerable forms, from neoCatharism, bogus psychological therapies, Rosicrucianism, to the gnostic Churches of California and elsewhere, appear to be sad, confused and partial manifestations of a philosophy which was (like all philosophy ultimately) never consistent with itself in the first place. Like the rest of us, Gnostics can seldom agree with each other as to whether this world is good or bad or, if both, how good and how bad. Is man his own saviour or not? Do we sin because we are essentially sinful or because it is impossible to do otherwise in a deficient world? If gnosis is superior to moral law should we look for moral qualities in the Godhead? The claims that Crowley made, for example, in presenting a system which in its highest orders is beyond 'division' or 'manifestation' – visible and invisible, idea and projection, right and wrong,

God and the devil etc. etc. do not appear to have furnished mankind with *adepti* who are truly interested in anything more than their own self-development. One can certainly find more men and women who give substance to the old appellation Divine, quietly living, largely unused, within the Church of England and in the other long-established religions. For a tradition which once claimed to represent the 'spirituals' of mankind, the fact that the fruits do not testify to the health of the tree is perhaps damning enough.

Nevertheless, there are, and will doubtless continue to be, lights in the darkness. If we are going to look at what gnosis has to say to our age then I don't think one need look far further than at the artist William Blake (1757–1827). Blake is a man for us. As a gnostic prophet of the Modern Age, there is to my knowledge no one to match him in penetrating insight, creative ability, simplicity of intent, goodness of character and in so many things profound understanding of what has happened to mankind since the advent of technological and scientific revolution in the late eighteenth century. It is right that we end our story of the Gnostics with 'English Blake', poet of a New Age.

Chapter Twelve

A Universe drained of God

Let us first return to the universe of Giordano Bruno. It is a divine and living universe, an infinite universe whose source is the divine intelligible world which eternally projects itself into, as it were, the divinized matter. The living 'forms' of God, the essential ideas of the universe can be glimpsed through abstract figures which, when firmly placed in the memory, enable the mind to see the true nature of the infinite universe.

But what if we limit perception from the divine *nous* of the gnostic to the 'mind of the ratio' – the rational mind observing objects in the universe? Then we may take the formulae of cosmic proportion as the real rather than as gateways to physical reality. The laws and formulae discernible through observation of matter enable man to predict and therefore to have power over nature. Is this not enough? Why bother with all that mystical trash? And what if we say that reality is out 'there' and that our minds are simply screens onto which the world projects itself; that the world exists to us only as sense impressions.

Then we would have objective knowledge – knowledge of objects. This became in the seventeenth and eighteenth centuries the aim of science. The result was a universe drained of God. Since God is invisible there is neither need nor possibility of examining Him. One would better content oneself with looking at matter. Any gnosis that may be is thrust to the 'outer limits' (to return perhaps as the 'Alien' of science fiction) – it cannot exist in the mind because the mind simply receives sense impressions. If we have a soul or conscience, it must be essentially separate from perception. If the universe is 'divine', then God can only be seen in the laws and mechanics which he has presumably created. These deductions from scientific observation (quantifiable and repeatable demonstration) were held in the eighteenth century to have brought clarity to a confused world. They are the origins of 'Deism'. 'Deism' holds that there is a God, He is a 'great architect', a designer, a mechanician. Everything can be shown as a mechanism. 'God' has long ago 'flicked a switch' and set the whole celestial machine in motion, sitting back to watch the process or perhaps He has departed to work on other projects. This view of God as 'creator' or in Isaac Newton's terms 'Pantocrator' is remarkably akin to the early Gnostic's view of the demiurge 'whose word is Law'. Isaac Newton's knowledge of the Gnostics is, however, slight. In an exceptionally rare work, *Observations upon the Prophecies of Daniel and the Apocalypse of Saint John. In two parts. 1733*, Isaac Newton, the father of gravity, writes:

> It (apostasy) began to work in the disciples of Simon, Menander, Carpocrates, Cerinthus, and such sorts of men as had imbibed the metaphysical philosophy of the Gentiles and Cabalistical Jews, and were thence called Gnosticks. John calls them Antichrists, saying that in his days there were many Antichrists.

Now they might be called 'anti-rationalists' – with reason! In the 'deist' view, God is held to be rational and rationality is held to be the proper road to understanding Man and his creator. But let us take another step. Since the universe runs itself and Man is the passive observer of it, imitating the mechanics of the universe, there is no real need for God at all – belief in God is simply a matter of taste, or of aesthetics. It is much simpler this way.

Let us take another view, that of Natural Religion. This view is the reaction of some theologians to the threats of a cosmology which has no need of God. The essence of this view is that God can be deduced from observing nature and, as such, is really a corollary of Deism. In William Paley's famous parable, we pick up a watch, it shows design, it shows rational structure – it must have a designer, likewise then the universe. The theologian thinks that he is saved from the abyss of atheism – God is good because nature is 'beautiful'.

William Blake attacked all of the above. He did not believe a word of it. For him, this whole movement which externalized nature 'separated the stars from the mountains, the mountains from Man And left Man, a little grovelling Root outside of Himself.' He held the culprits to be Bacon, Newton and Locke. These were, for Blake, the servants of materialism. When we hear the word 'materialism', we might think that it implies a critique of our civilization, in that people are acquisitive; they want things, they value things, they study things, they produce things, they exchange things, they work for things, they die for things, they kill for things, they dominate things – a man is a thing with a personality which may have greater or lesser material value – and the blood which keeps all the things in motion is money. The word is sometimes tied to 'capitalism' – the exchange of things for profit.

In fact, materialism is much more fundamental a concept, and all the above are in a sense only symptoms or rather effects of it. Materialism means that the source of all things is matter and should we go back far enough to when matter 'was not', then there would be nothing, absolutely nothing – because there can be no thing without matter. And Man has evolved from this nothing.

Our civilisation may not actually believe in materialism but it certainly acts as if it did. There is a further point to consider before we approach the subject of Blake's vision. One may call it the 'myth of Frankenstein'.

Man the Monster

In Chapter 2 of Mary Shelley's novel *Frankenstein*, written when Blake was 59, we hear of the beginnings of Victor Frankenstein's quest to attain the powers of a god. Victor confesses that during a trip to Thonon, a town near the French Alps situated by the shores of Lake Léman:

> I chanced to find a volume of the works of Cornelius Agrippa. I opened it with apathy; the theory which he attempts to demonstrate [from the *Asclepius* – that of Hermetic Man bringing life into inanimate objects], and the wonderful facts which he relates, soon changed this feeling into enthusiasm. A new light seemed to dawn upon my mind; and, bounding with joy, I communicated my discovery to my father. My father looked carelessly at the title page of my book, and said 'Ah! Cornelius Agrippa! My dear Victor, do not waste your time upon this; it is sad trash.'
>
> If, instead of this remark, my father had taken the pains to explain to me, that the principles of Agrippa had been entirely exploded, and that a modern system of science had been introduced, which possessed much greater powers than the ancient, because the powers of the latter were chimerical, while those of the former were real and practical; under such circumstances, I should certainly have thrown Agrippa aside, and having contented my imagination, warmed as it was, by returning with greater ardour to my former studies. It is even possible, that the train of my ideas would never have received the fatal impulse that led to my ruin. But the cursory glance my father had taken of my volume by no means assured me that he was acquainted with its contents; and I continued to read with the greatest avidity.

At Ingolstadt University, Frankenstein met the 'uncouth' Professor Krempe who echoed his father's disapprobation: 'Every instant that you have wasted on those books is utterly and entirely lost.... I little expected, in this enlightened and scientific age, to find a disciple of

Albertus Magnus and Paracelsus.' The latter men were alchemists of noetic character – men of the *nous*. Frankenstein was upset and complained, 'I was required to exchange chimeras of boundless magnitude for realities of little worth.' Nevertheless, on encountering the more kindly Professor Waldman, he saw new possibilities. Waldman is more positive about Hermetic alchemy:

'The ancient teachers of this science,' said he, 'promised impossibilities, and performed nothing. The modern masters promise very little; they know that metals cannot be transmuted, and that the elixir of life is a chimera. But these philosophers, whose hands seem only made to dabble in dirt, and their eyes to pore over the microscope or crucible, have indeed performed miracles.'

At this point, paradoxically, Waldman proceeds to paraphrase from Pico della Mirandola's Oratio:

They penetrate into the recesses of nature, and show how she works in her hiding places. They ascend into the heavens: they have discovered how the blood circulates, and the nature of the air we breathe. They have acquired new and almost unlimited powers; they can command the thunders of heaven, mimic the earthquake, and even mock the invisible world with its own shadows.

As for Cornelius Agrippa and his type:

... these were men to whose indefatigable zeal modern philosophers were indebted for most of the foundations of their knowledge. They had left to us, as an easier task, to give new names, and arrange in connected classifications, the facts which they in a great degree had been the instruments of bringing to light. The labours of men of genius, however erroneously directed, scarcely ever fail in ultimately turning to the solid advantage of mankind.

Two points can be deduced from these rather pompous speeches. The first is inherent to the text, that is, that the 'old sixteenth-century Hermetic vision' is reported in the novel to have inspired the work of natural scientists – and this accords with what we have understood in the last section of the imaginative power of Hermetism.

The second point is that which leads to the central tragedy of the book – Frankenstein's creation of the 'monster'. Frankenstein is encouraged by Waldman – although Waldman is ignorant that this is what he has done – to fuse the visionary scape of the Agrippan magus with the methods of natural science. The result of this powerful drive in Frankenstein's mind is to attempt the ultimate act of science as he sees it – to create life itself, to do the work of the Creator. In gnostic terms,

Frankenstein has become a demiurge, an 'archon', a ruler over nature, heedless to Nature's spiritual source. We may say that he has taken the knowledge of nature and confused this knowledge with that of the eternal or 'occult', hidden nature of which Agrippa wrote. All that can come from this is hideous deformity, and on realizing his colossal error of hubris Frankenstein finds himself to be 'a grovelling Root, outside of himself'. Filled with unspeakable remorse, Frankenstein laments that:

> Now all was blasted: instead of that serenity of conscience, which allowed me to look back upon the past with self-satisfaction, and from thence to gather promise of new hopes, I was seized by remorse and the sense of guilt, which hurried me away to a hell of intense tortures such as no language can describe.

Later he will declare, 'I am a blasted tree; the bolt has entered my soul; and I felt then that I should survive to exhibit, what I shall soon cease to be – a miserable spectacle of wrecked humanity, pitiable to others, and intolerable to myself.' Like Samuel Taylor Coleridge's 'Ancient Mariner', who is condemned because he has broken the invisible laws of nature by shooting the 'albatross', Frankenstein too must survive awhile to show us the horror of man's 'new' predicament. Frankenstein and the Mariner have become outsiders, alone – and Mary Shelley employs the lurid language of the 'romantic hell' to emphasize the sense of foreboding for a future in which, stalking across a Godless landscape in an empty universe, it is Man that will be shown to be more monstrous than his creations.

Coleridge in his poetic *tour de force*, 'The Ryme of the Ancient Mariner' paints the picture of a possible future for mankind, blinded by power:

> Alone, alone, all all alone
> Alone on the wide wide Sea;
> And Christ would take no pity on
> My soul in agony.
>
> The many men so beautiful,
> And they all dead did lie!
> And a million million slimy things
> Lived on – and so did I.
>
> I looked upon the rotting Sea,
> And drew my eyes away;
> I looked upon the ghastly deck,
> And there the dead men lay.

> I looked to heaven, and tried to pray;
> But or ever a prayer had gusht,
> A wicked whisper came and made
> My heart as dry as dust.

Today, we should not be far from the author's understanding if we saw the above as a vision of the effects of ecological holocaust. Samuel Taylor Coleridge (1772–1834), genius of prose and poetry, is reported to have met William Blake by the critic Crabb Robinson in 1826, and by an anonymous writer in the *London University Magazine* for 1830, three years after Blake's death. In a footnote, the writer describes how: 'Blake and Coleridge, when in company, seemed like congenial beings of another sphere, breathing for a while on our earth; which may be easily perceived from the similarity of thought pervading their works.'

'Like congenial beings of another sphere.' Both men had seen the 'monster' on the horizon of their own hearts and both men had seen how the monster might yet be redeemed.

Chapter Thirteen

Thou also dwellest in Eternity

God is in the lowest effects as well as in the highest causes
(William Blake)

I spoke to the distinguished biographer of Blake, Dr Kathleen Raine, in the spring of 1986 and she began by saying that: 'If you start from mind or spirit being the basic, fundamental reality, you have a whole field illuminated which is totally closed if you assume matter to be the basic reality.' That field was illuminated by the vision of William Blake (1757–1827).

William Blake was born over the hosiery shop of his father, James Blake at 28, Broad Street, Golden Square in London, in 1757. Young William very early on distinguished himself by his strong character, a character which seemed to have a full sense of its own integrity. In *Infant Sorrow* from his *Songs of Experience*, he wrote of his birth, as if already a conscious being:

> My mother groaned, my father wept:
> Into the dangerous world I leapt,
> Helpless, naked, piping loud,
> Like a fiend hid in a cloud.

His birth was in his own eyes an 'incarnation'. He had come from eternity, from immortal form into a world of generation. He would go on to cavil at the confusion of reality with appearance, spirit with matter: 'Truly,' he declared to the Devil of Selfhood (Ego), 'thou art a dunce who does not know the garment from the man.' Coming into the world was a most unpleasant experience:

> Striving against my swaddling bands,
> Bound and weary, I thought best
> To sulk upon my mother's breast.

He would come to see that the world of generation was not without its purpose but served to effect the 'Marriage of Heaven and Hell' – to rebuild the fallen citadel of the 'Divine Humanity'. In the book *Jerusalem* (1804) he employed the Smaragdine Table of Hermes Trismegistus: 'What is above is like that which is below. To work the miracle of the one thing.' Heaven and Hell, between which the world is poised, will be united.

When he was four, Blake screamed at seeing 'God put his forehead to the window'. He would recall straying into the fields of Peckham Rye where he passed a tree full of angels, their bright wings shining in the boughs. On one summer's day his mother found cause to beat him because he related how he had seen the prophet Ezekiel sitting in the open fields. His father, noticing William's anger at being beaten, wisely saw that school was no place for him and so William educated himself – as he continued to do for the rest of his seventy years.

Throughout his life he kept himself and later his beloved wife Catherine by the exercise of his engraving skills which he learned as an apprentice to James Basire at 31, Great Queen Street. He lived in London for almost all of his life and he never left the country. Blake seems, in the main, to have found London to be an agreeable place and in his day it was a very much smaller place than it is today. The phrase Greater London would only have implied the wealth of intellectual, pecuniary and artistic ferment which existed there in those days. You could see a kingfisher where Euston Station now stands.

Blake was gifted with an exceptionally strong visionary faculty and when we talk of vision, let us be in no doubt as to what it means. Vision means to see, really see – not 'with the eye', the 'vegetable eye', but through it. To see reality is vision. It is the visual counterpart of 'intellect': *nous*. The mind is creative of reality – the mind is not a blank screen. The individual can share in the vision of the eternal form of humanity – humanity itself. Individuals share their source in the divine being. So when Blake wanders down the streets of London, he does not see simply the passing shades and images of people. It is not objects he sees but:

> In every cry of every man,
> In every infant's cry of fear,
> In every voice, in every ban,
> The mind-forged manacles I hear.
>
> How the chimney-sweeper's cry
> Every blackening church appals,
> And the hapless soldier's sigh
> Runs in blood from palace-walls.

Blake sees the inner reality – he cannot avoid it because he knows that the outer world is created within our Imagination, and for Blake, the 'Divine Imagination' is all. If our minds are shackled, we show ourselves to be downcast and unhappy, miserable and given to mistreatment, perverse in thought and action – we shut out the divine vision and all about us we 'see' only objects separated by dismal space. Blake believed the science and religion of his time encouraged the appearance of the 'mind-forged manacles'. They trusted appearances.

Blake dia*gnosed* and understood the mental imprisonment of Englishmen and women. He may have remained in London, but as a creative artist, his range of vision was, like Bruno's, infinite:

> I travelled through a land of men
> A land of men and women too,
> And heard and saw such dreadful things
> As cold earth wanderers never knew.
> ('The Mental Traveller')

Blake knew. He understood those principles of microcosm and macrocosm and of nous and matter which he gleaned from his deep reading of Plato, the NeoPlatonists, the Hermetica, Dante, the Bible and it is likely he knew about a Gnostic papyrus from the fourth or fifth century, discovered by James Bruce in Upper Egypt and deposited in the British Museum in 1785. It was called *Pistis Sophia*, 'Faith-Wisdom', the name given to the revealer of gnostic vision to Christ's disciples on the Mount of Olives after the Resurrection of Jesus Christ. Blake attended the lectures of Thomas Taylor 'the Platonist' which took place in the home of his friend, the sculptor Flaxman. Taylor translated Plato, Proclus, Plotinus, Iamblichus and other Neoplatonists. Blake loved these works. Above all, it can be seen that Blake was gnostic.

> The Vision of Christ that thou dost see,
> Is my vision's greatest enemy.
> Thine is the Friend of all Mankind,
> Mine speaks in Parables to the blind.
> Thine loves the same world that mine hates,
> Thy heaven doors are my hell gates.
> ('The Everlasting Gospel')

I asked Kathleen Raine about his being gnostic and she replied:

People thought – and W. B. Yeats gave currency to the idea – that Blake had made it all up; that he was a mystic, whatever that is – he wasn't. He was a gnostic. You're quite right. It was gnosis. It wasn't mysticism. He was a gnostic and he was enormously deeply read. I thought I'd start out by reading everything he is known to have read – twenty years later I'm still reading! I followed that golden string to a whole excluded knowledge.

Of that 'golden string', Blake wrote in his consummate poetic achievement, 'Jerusalem':

> I give you the end of a golden string:
> Only wind it into a ball, –
> It will lead you in at Heaven's gate,
> Built in Jersualem's wall.

Kathleen Raine comments:

> ... it is the same thread. It proved not to be a whole lot of dubious occult writers but proved essentially to be the NeoPlatonists, the Gnostics, the Alchemical tradition – Goethe and Jung picked up the alchemical tradition – Jacob Boehme (fifteenth-century German Gnostic) – as Blake did in England, the Neoplatonic tradition. Blake had also read the *Hermetica*, Thomas Taylor the Platonist – the translator of Plato and Plotinus. All Blake's so-called system was built up on very well grounded, and usually very respectable knowledge of the excluded tradition.

Blake was confident that he stood on solid ground, a long tradition which had proved its worth – the deists and rationalists could never defeat the Divine Imagination – for we come from it, that is to say, the eternal forms create us, not the reverse. So:

> Mock on, mock on, Voltaire, Rousseau,
> Mock on, mock on; 'tis all in vain;
> You throw the dust against the wind,
> And the wind blows it back again
> ('Scoffers')

We all know the hymn 'Jerusalem' which exclaims, 'And did those feet in ancient time...'. In fact it comes from Blake's 'Milton' but no matter. When we sing the second verse:

> And did the Countenance Divine
> Shine forth upon our clouded hills?
> And was Jerusalem builded here
> Among those dark Satanic mills?

perhaps we have been accustomed to imagine that the 'dark satanic mills' represent those rows upon rows of Coronation Streets; always black and white and condemned by funnels of hellish smoke. Perhaps we see shaky images of Jarrow marchers and the hollow cheeks of the 'urban poor'. Blake was, in fact, referring to his time spent at Felpham as the guest of a popular poet of the day, William Hayley. Here Blake was encouraged to paint screens and fans and the kind of 'sound' engraving that was accessible to Hayley's mind. For Blake, the 'dark Satanic mills' are symbols of confined and meaningless labour, the repressed vision of man, so haunted by propriety. But those who see the industrial landscape are really quite right. The intuition is good because the dark world of industrial mechanism is in Blake's thought nothing less than the outflow of the repressed vision wreaking a kind of vengeance on Nature. 'What is above is like that which is below.' An empty head will produce empty works. An abstracted architect will produce abstracted, angular, lifeless buildings – mental prisons for people. As Christ said, 'First clean the inside of the cup.' The cup of the mind of the new Industrial Revolution was already shattered to Blake's vision. Listen to how Blake describes the effect of industrial capitalism – so much more profound than the Marxian critique; for it penetrates the soul of Man, bound, torn and stretched about the mechanistic creations of Reason:

> All the Arts of Life they chang'd into the Arts of Death in Albion.
> The hour-glass contemn'd because its simple workmanship
> Was like the workmanship of the plowman, and the water wheel
> That raises water into cisterns, broken and burn'd with fire
> Because its workmanship was like the workmanship of the shepherd;
> And in their stead, intricate wheels invented, wheel without wheel,
> To perplex youth in their outgoings and to bind to labours in Albion
> Of day and night the myriads of eternity; that they may grind
> and polish brass and iron hour after hour, laborious task,
> Kept ignorant of its use: that they might spend the days of wisdom
> In sorrowful drudgery to obtain a scanty pittance of bread,
> In ignorance to view a small portion and think that All,
> And call it Demonstration, blind to all the simple rules of life.

Is it so very different today? In 1983 I wrote that:

> The Computer Cottage is an electric prison
> Welded
> In the Fear of Vision.

But how was hell made so well on earth?

In Blake's series of astonishing myths – imaginative representations of inner psycho spiritual activity – laid out in a series of 'Prophetic Books', Blake told the story of the fall of Divine Humanity. These are timeless myths in their essentials but we can place the dynamics of the tragedy within the context of the previous chapter: 'The Universe drained of God', or as Blake described it: 'The soul-shuddering vacuum of Newtonian space' – the development of materialism. As for 'Space', Blake wrote in 'Milton':

> Every space larger than a red globule of man's blood
> Is visionary, and is created by the hammer of Los.
> And every space smaller than a globule of man's blood opens
> Into eternity, of which the vegetable earth is but a shadow.

Space is a creation of Imagination. Of course, like time it is relative. I discussed Blake's response to materialism with Kathleen Raine:

> He held materialism to be totally false. Not in its conclusions but in its premises. He believed man to be a spiritual being in a spiritual universe, which was a living universe, not a mechanism as the Newtonians supposed. He held the whole universe to be alive and to be also living within the spiritual unity of the being, the person he called the Divine Humanity – named *Albion*. He saw the spiritual universe to be a person – he said of Pythagoras: 'God is not a spiritual diagram.' God is a person, He is the Divine Humanity, he is Jesus the Imagination. W. B. Yeats took off where Blake left off and identified this figure with the 'Self' of the Upanishads.

In the *Book of Urizen* (1793), the drama takes place within. The *unus mundus* – the 'one world' contains both the inner and the outer worlds in a single life. Blake says quite distinctly that although it appears 'without', it is within – in the Imagination. I mention the *Book of Urizen* and readers may be perplexed. Who or what is 'Urizen'? Urizen is Blake's mythic figure representing 'Reason', abstract, cold and blind – the 'mind of the ratio' as a living principle.

The drama of fall and redemption which Blake expresses in a series of Prophetic Books occurs within the mind of Albion. 'Albion' is the 'Ancient Man' who contained in himself all things: 'The primeval state of man was wisdom, art, and science.' He is certainly akin to the Valentinian Anthrōpos – the projection of eternity, and to the Cabalist's 'Adam Kadmon'. He is the original form of Man, Divine Humanity. Albion's body we may see as 'England's green and pleasant land' for Albion is the spiritual form of England. One must try to imagine 'England' as a single being – in whom all the events of the body of England are but events deriving from the inner life. 'Albion' is the being to whom Jerusalem – spiritual liberty calls:

> England! awake! awake! awake!
> Jerusalem thy sister calls!
> Why wilt thou sleep the sleep of death,
> And close her from thy ancient walls.

Albion is a fallen being. How did this happen?

Within the 'ancient Man' there existed, prior to the tragedy, four principles, four eternal projections called 'Zoas', living within harmonious mind. They are *Reason* (Urizen), *Feeling* (called 'Luvah' which is Love), *Sensation* (which is called 'Tharmas', or the body) and *Intuition* (who is called 'Los' who did not fall but kept the Divine Vision in time of doubt as 'Poetry, Painting and Music, the three powers in man of conversing with Pardise which the flood [of Time and Space] did not sweep away.').

In English civilization the one of the four faculties which has really led us astray has been fallen Reason who by usurping the harmony of mind, declaring as does the gnostic demiurge in the Apocryphon of John, 'There is no god before me', is responsible for cutting us off from our spiritual source. Within the spiritual being, Urizen is responsible for the fall of the West. It should be noted that Blake lived to hear of how the goddess 'Reason' was erected in Notre Dame during the wicked events of the French Revolution. Blake does identify Urizen as the essential nature of the 'second God' of Plato and the Gnostics. He is recognizably the 'Elohim' of the Old Testament in his 'aged ignorance', carrying the books of the Law. Yet, and yet Blake's creator is not wholly evil; for as the 'Ancient of Days' on the frontispiece to *Europe* (1793) we see the Creator with his golden compasses, who, though in part fallen, 'derived his birth from the supreme God; this being fell, by degrees, from his native virtue, and his primitive dignity' (W. B. Yeats). But whatever the grandeur of his work, Blake called the creator of the temporal world 'a very cruel being'. Who can deny this, waking from a nightmare which convinced us a loved one was dead, that emptiness, emptiness . . .

> A murderer of its own body, but also a murderer
> Of every Divine Member. It is the reasoning power,
> An abstract objecting power that negatives every-thing.
> This is the spectre of man, the holy reasoning power,
> And in its holiness is closed the Abomination of Desolation.
> (from 'Jerusalem')

Urizen is responsible for the crushing laws of both science and religion For in Blake's day, the Church had become rationalized showing a slavish adherence to the fantasies of 'enlightened' science, unaware of the spiritual treasure within it, the Glory of God. It is Urizen who says 'Thou shalt not':

I went to the Garden of Love,
And saw what I never had seen,
A Chapel was built in the midst,
Where I used to play on the green.

And the gates of this Chapel were shut,
And 'Thou shalt not' writ over the door;
So I turned to the Garden of Love
That so many sweet flowers bore.

And I saw it was filled with graves,
And tombstones where flowers should be;
And priests in black gowns were walking their rounds,
And binding with briars my joys and desires.

('The Garden of Love')

Urizen is the God of the deists and 'natural religionists' and Blake calls him 'Old Nobodaddy' to whom he addresses these lines:

Why art thou silent and invisible,
Father of Jealousy?
Why dost thou hide thyself in clouds
From every searching eye?
Why darkness and obscurity
In all thy words and laws,

The fall of Reason is, within the living mind, responsible for the mechanical abstract consciousness that analyses, that is, 'loosens' or 'breaks apart'. What happens when this consciousness is brought to bear on the natural world? Then the world is seen as a kind of cake or diagram – 5 per cent uranium, 30 per cent copper, 20 per cent oil, 45 per cent iron-ore and so on – there to be divided; the consciousness of Man ripped to pieces on the analyst's couch of a confused world. The poet cannot speak, or paint, or write, make films, debate or be without the question, 'But what does it mean?' In 'Jerusalem' Blake gets to the heart of the matter:

Why wilt thou number every little fibre of my soul,
Spreading them out before the sun like stalks of flax to dry?
The infant joy is beautiful, but its anatomy
Horrible, ghast, and deadly. Nought shalt thou find in it
But dark despair and everlasting brooding melancholy.

('Analysis')

Within the general disorder of Albion's mind, Feeling, 'Luvah' also falls and in the fallen state is called 'Orc', child of freedom and rebellion, chained to the rock of the Law, Promethean Love on fire! Orc is frustrated Love and love frustrated falls into violence, being blood-thirsty, destructive and warlike: 'when thought is closed in chains then Love shall show its roots in deepest hell'. Within the Divine Being, there is darkness too. Evil has its part to play – but not for Man. Orc is much in evidence today, from bloody terror to, in Kathleen Raine's eyes, 'Orc manifesting himself in football hooliganism and in the poor little punk children on the King's Road.'

Within Blake's triumphant poetic synthesis 'Jerusalem' (1804) the four faculties or Zoas are reunited. Jung might call this 'individuation' but Blake saw it in more cosmic terms and images than that. Urizen is redeemed and reincorporated into the true body of 'Jesus the Imagination' and Albion, Humanity, expansive and divine is revealed once more. When Reason is obedient to his true but hitherto unknown source in the Divine Imagination, he appears in his proper form, not as false god but as the 'sower and reaper of eternity', the mental binding power which ensures coherence within the Mind. Albion may again dwell in Jerusalem which is nothing less than what this present world cannot bear – spiritual liberty!

> In Great Eternity every particular form gives forth or emanates
> Its own peculiar light, and the form is the Divine Vision,
> And the light is His garment. This is Jerusalem in every man,
> A tent and tabernacle of mutual forgiveness, male and female clothings.
> And Jerusalem is called Liberty among the children of Albion.

All of this came to Blake as spiritual knowledge; heart and intellect, all nature's vision combined in mind and synthesized in sight. If any should condemn this knowledge, Blake speaks thus:

> He who despises and mocks a mental gift in another, calling it pride, and selfishness, and sin, mocks Jesus, the giver of every mental gift, which always appear to the ignorance-loving hypocrite as sins. But that which is a sin in the sight of cruel man is not so in the sight of our kind God. Let every Christian as much as in him lies, engage himself openly and publicly before all the world in some mental pursuit for the building of Jerusalem.

Eternity in an Hour

As in Bruno we see the full dimensions of the outer world of gnostic perception, so in Blake we are reunited with the inner world.

In 1827, Blake wrote to a friend:

> I have been very near the gates of death, and have returned very weak, and an old man, feeble and tottering, but not in spirit and life, not in the

149

real man, the imagination which liveth forever. In that I grow stronger and stronger as this foolish body decays.

'The death of a saint' said a poor woman who came to help Mrs Blake. Surrounded on his bed by his unfinished work on Dante's *Paradiso*, he composed songs to his Maker so sweetly to the ear of his wife that she drew nearer to him. He looked at her with great affection and said: 'My beloved! They are not mine. No! They are not mine.' He told her that they would not be parted, that 'the ruins of time build mansions in eternity'. He died in Fountain Court in 1827.

In his 'Everlasting Gospel' William Blake had God speak thus to Christ:

> If thou humblest thyself, thou humblest Me.
> Thou also dwellest in eternity.
> Thou art a man. God is no more.
> Thine own humanity learn to adore;
> For that is my spirit of life.

Appendix One

Chronology

c. 427–347 BC	Lifetime of Plato.
c. AD 30	Crucifixion of Jesus of Nazareth.
c. 30–60	Activity of Paul.
c. 50	Simon Magus in Samaria.
c. 70–80	Composition of Gospels of Luke and Matthew.
c. 90–100	Composition of *Gospel of John*.
c. 100?	Original form of *Apocryphon of John*.
	Jewish Esotericism – Merkabah (Throne) Mysticism.
c. 120–130	Carpocrates in Alexandria(?) Basic elements of some Nag Hammadi works: *Exegesis on the soul*; *Sophia of Jesus Christ*; *Apocalypse of Adam*; *Hypostasis of the Archons*; *Gospel of Thomas*; *Apocryphon of James*; *Apocalypses of James*.
c. 130	Gnostics in Rome.
143	Expulsion of Valentinus from Church in Rome.
c. 150?	Formulation of *Poimandres* (Corpus Hermeticum I).
c. 150–215	Clement of Alexandria.
c. 150–225	Tertullian
c. 150	*The Golden Ass* – autobiographical novel of Apuleius of Madaura; describes mystical initiation into cult of Isis.
c. 160	Death of Valentinus.
177	Persecution of Christians instigated by Marcus Aurelius Caesar. Martyrs of Lyon and Vienne.
180	Composition of *Refutation and Subversion of knowledge falsely so-called*, by Bishop Irenaeus of Lyons.
205–270	Plotinus, Neoplatonist philosopher. In his *Enneads* he writes against Gnostics who condemn the world. Being distant from the source of divine being, we should not be surprised at imperfection of world, argues Plotinus. Some Gnostic Hermetists in basic agreement with this.
216	Mani born in Babylonia.
c. 228	First vision of Mani.

240	Mani receives call to be 'Apostle of Light'.
c. 320	Founding of Coptic monasteries by Pachomius.
325	Creed of Nicaea defines orthodox belief at instigation of Emperor Constantine I.
c. 350	Nag Hammadi Codices collected.
356	Athanasius in hiding among monks of Upper Egypt.
361–363	Reign of Emperor Julian the Apostate, who attempted to revive paganism with solar symbolism as a unifying factor.
367	Theodore, head of Pachomian monastery at Tabinnisi near Nag Hammadi, instructed to read 39th Festal letter of Athanasius, Bishop of Alexandria which condemns heretical books. Possible time of burial of Nag Hammadi Codices.
373–382	Augustine of Hippo a Manichee 'hearer'.
375–395	Under Emperor Theodosius I, being a Manichee carries the death penalty.
719	A Manichee church is built in Peking.
762–840	Manicheism is the state religion of the Uigurs (Chotsko).
834–844	Persecution of Manichees in China.
872	Military victory over Paulicians of Armenia; many of them move to Balkans.
c. 950	Activity of the Bogomil (Beloved of God) in Bulgaria.
1120	Anti-Manichean edict in China.
1163	Assembly of Catholic bishops at Tours recommends stern measures against the Cathars of Gascony and Provence.
c. 1172	Cathar council of St. Félix de Caraman, headed by Nicetas from Constantinople.
	Dominic Guzman born at Caleruaga in Castile.
1190	Pope Alexander III pronounces Cathars to be anathema.
1203	Arnold Amaury and Peter of Castelnau, Papal Legates on mission to convert Cathars and to ensure nobles take action against them.
c. 1204	Raymond de Péreille rebuilds château of Montségur at request of local Cathars.
1206	Dominic begins conversion mission, based at Prouille. Esclarmonde of Foix receives Consolamentum from Guilhabert de Castres at great gathering of lords at Fanjeaux.
1207	Dominic Guzman and Guilhabert de Castres debate in Montréal.
1208	15 January – Papal Legate, Peter of Castelnau cut down by troops of Raymond VI of Toulouse at St. Gilles. Pope Innocent III issues call to arms. End of Dominic's main conversion mission.
1209	Army commanded by Simon de Montfort assembles at Lyon.

1210	Siege of Minerve, 22 July. 140 Cathar *perfecti* burned at stake.
1215	The Dominican Order of Friar Preachers founded.
1217	First 'Albigensian Crusade' ends.
1217–1258	Mongol conquests in Central and Western Asia; end of Manichean communities.
1220	Guilhabert de Castres 'Bishop' of Cathar diocese of Toulouse.
1221	Dominic Guzman dies.
1226	Crusade against Cathars led by King of France, Louis VIII. (Saint Louis).
1233	Dominican Order granted right to inquisition by Pope.
1243–44	Siege of Montségur.
1244	16 March, 225 Cathar *perfecti* burned at stake at Montségur.
1271	Languedoc passes under French crown.
1321	Bélibaste – last Cathar to be burned at Villerouge-Termènes.
1460	Leonardo of Pistoia brings Greek manuscript of *Corpus Hermeticum* to Florence from Macedonia.
1463	Giovanni Pico, count of Mirandola, is born.
1471	First printed edition of Ficino's Latin translation of *Divine Pymander* appears.
1486	Pico writes his *Oratio* as introduction to 900 Theses to be debated in Florence. Henry Cornelius Agrippa of Nettesheim is born.
1487	4 August, Pope Innocent VIII pronounces 13 of these theses to be heretical. Pico flees.
1494	Pico dies. He is thirty-one.
1533	Agrippa publishes his Three Books of Occult Philosophy.
1535	Henry Cornelius Agrippa dies.
1543	Publication of *On the Revolutions of the Celestial Orbs* by Copernicus.
1548	Giordano Bruno born at Nola by Vesuvius.
1564	John Dee publishes his *Monas Hieroglyphica* at Antwerp.
1583	Giordano Bruno publishes his *On the Infinite Universe and Worlds*.
1600	Bruno burnt at the stake in Rome as an 'impenitent heretic'.
1608	John Dee dies at Mortlake.
1614	Isaac Casaubon proves that the *Corpus Hermeticum* was written in late antiquity and is not therefore pre-Christian. Rosicrucian Manifestos begin to appear with the *Fama Fraternitas*. Attracts widespread interest.
1615	*Confessio Fraternitatis*, Rosicrucian Manifesto appears.
1616	*The Chemical Wedding*, another Rosicrucian manifesto

appears. Intimations in manifestos of scientific enlightenment to come of gnostic character.

1618–1624   Jacob Boehme, German shoemaker writing vast array of intuitively Gnostic works with strong affinities to Jewish Kabbalah.

17–18th   Formation in Europe of Lodges of 'Freemasons' promising
centuries   illumination of cosmic mysteries. Runs underground of main movements of rationalist 'enlightenment'. Speedy developments of mechanical and chemical science.

1757   William Blake born in London.

1785   Gnostic manuscript *Pistis Sophia* deposited in British Museum, from fourth or fifth century, discovered by James Bruce in Luxor. Likely that Blake knew of the discovery.

1793   Blake issues *The Book of Urizen*.

1804   Blake issues his epic poem *Jerusalem*.

1816   Mary Shelley writes first draft of *Frankenstein*.

1827   William Blake dies.

1875   Theosophical Society founded by Madame H. P. Blavatsky and others.

   Edward Alexander (Aleister) Crowley born in Leamington.

1890s   Formation of Hermetic Order of Golden Dawn, headed by L. MacGregor Mathers.

1934   Hans Jonas completes Vol. I of *Gnosis und spätantiker geist* (Gnosis and the spirit of late antiquity).

1945   Muḥammad⸍Alī al-Sammān and his brothers discover the 'Nag Hammadi Library' at Hamra Dūm in Upper Egypt (December).

1952   Gilles Quispel obtains Codex I (Jung Codex) from a middleman in Brussels for 35,000 Swiss francs.

1955   First major description of discovery: *The Jung Codex. A newly recovered Gnostic papyrus* by G. Quispel and H. C. Puech.

1958   Jean Doresse publishes *The Secret Books of the Egyptian Gnostics* with the first published translation of *The Gospel of Thomas*, in French.

   The Gnostic Religion by Hans Jonas published.

1959   *The Gospel of Thomas* published in English.

1966   Colloquium on Origins of Gnosticism held at Messina takes up initiative of Professor James M. Robinson and others to press ahead with publication of entire Nag Hammadi Library.

1970   James Marshall Hendrix, musician and composer dies in London. A few hours before dying he writes in a last lyric: 'The story is written/by so many people who dared,/to lay down the truth/to so very many who cared/to carry the cross/of Jesus and beyond/We will gild the light/this time with a woman/in our arms.'

1971	James Douglas Morrison, composer and poet, dies in Paris.
1972	First photographic edition of Nag Hammadi Library available.
1975	'Jung Codex' (Codex I) 'returned' to the Coptic Museum, Cairo, where lies the Nag Hammadi Library.
1977	E. J. Brill of Leiden publish the *Nag Hammadi Library in English* which is edited by Professor James M. Robinson and translated by a 'group' of international scholars.
1980	John Lennon shot to death in New York City.
1984	Library of J. R. Ritman institutionalized in Amsterdam, the *Bibliotheca Philosophica Hermetica* which contains the story of the Gnosis in first editions and modern works.
1987	Television series on the subject of the Gnosis is made for Channel 4 Television in UK, 1,620 years after the order to read the 39th Festal Letter of Bishop Athanasius of Alexandria, condemning heretical books.

Appendix Two

The Nag Hammadi Library

Contains 13 codices (books), the first eleven of which were bound in leather covers. Codex 13 contains only sixteen pages which were slipped into another codex before the discovery. Codex 12 is also very thin and it would seem that Muḥammad ⸗ Alī's mother may have burned the remainder if it had not already been lost at the time of the discovery. Readers who wish to examine the contents in their fullness are advised to gain access to a copy of *The Nag Hammadi Library*, translated into English under the Editorship of James M. Robinson, published by E. J. Brill of Leiden.

There follows a list of the contents of the library with a very brief note as to their contents. Those texts quoted in this book are marked by an asterisk.

Codex One (The 'Jung Codex')

1. *Prayer of the Apostle Paul*
   A pseudonymous prayer attributed to Paul employing echoes of New Testament language. Paul asks Jesus Christ to 'redeem my eternal light-soul and spirit'.
2. *The Apocryphon of James**
   Apocryphon means a secret book and this one conveys secret teaching given by the Saviour to the Apostle James after the Resurrection.
3. *The Gospel of Truth**
   A beautiful and poetic work by an unnamed Gnostic teacher, thought to be Valentinus by some scholars. The writer expounds the meaning of Jesus' life and death. The work contains the famous 'nightmare passage' which is quoted at the beginning of Chapter Two of this book. The Gnostic emerges from a world of paranoiac illusion into the pure realm of spirit and consciousness.
4. *The Treatise on the Resurrection*
   A Valentinian work also known as the 'Letter to Rheginos' expounds the spiritual meaning of the resurrection: 'What, then, is the resurrection ... it is more fitting to say that the world is an illusion, rather than the resurrection which has come into being through Our Lord the Saviour.'

5. *The Tripartite Tractate*

Contents show some kinship to the thought of the Valentinian school. A difficult work which attempts to incorporate thought on the creation of human beings, spiritual reality and the three-fold division of men into *hylic* (material), *psychic* (unperfected spirit) and *pneumatic* (spiritual) types.

Codex Two

1. *The Apocryphon of John**

A work of this name was known to Irenaeus. It is in a sense a Gnostic commentary on the first chapters of Genesis and it rejects the 'Elohim' (a name given to God in Genesis) as being a deceiver of men who with his archons has blinded man from knowledge of his true identity. Man was made to 'drink water of forgetfulness'. The Saviour wakes people up and is able to defeat the amnesia-inducing operation of 'Yaltabaoth' (God of Genesis). Things are 'not as Moses said' (Moses was thought to have written Genesis).

2. *The Gospel of Thomas**

An important collection of sayings attributed to the 'living Jesus', some of which are very like sayings of Jesus in the New Testament and it may be that some of them are contemporaneous with canonical gospel sources.

3. *The Gospel of Philip**

Like the other 'gospels' in the collection, they convey 'good news' for the Gnostic but do not convey information about the *life* of Jesus prior to the Resurrection. This gospel contains much philosophy and many pleasing or interesting aphorisms suggesting a highly tuned mind on the part of the author who is also blessed with humour. Some might say it is a clever work by a know-all – and perhaps the author would be flattered. 'Adam came into being from two virgins, from the Spirit and from the virgin earth. Christ, therefore, was born from a virgin to rectify the fall which occurred in the beginning.' Only when the light flows forth from all shall the slaves be free.

4. *The Hypostasis of the Archons (Reality of the Rulers)*

The Gnostics were in no doubt as to 'who was running the show'. The Archons want to keep the Light to themselves or stamp it out altogether – which they cannot do. The Archons, ruled by 'Samael' or 'Sakla' (Fool) are held to be very real and their existence casts a pall over temporal life – but they will not last. The Children of the Light will be set free.

5. *On the Origin of the World*

Originally untitled, this work conforms to the title given to it The Gnostic world-view is laid out in essay form.

6. *The Exegesis on the Soul*

A mythology of the journey via degradation of the soul. 'Wise men of old gave the soul a feminine name.' The soul is made prostitute to the world but can be redeemed. The treatise contains quotations from the Old and New Testaments and from the Odyssey of Homer.

7. *The Book of Thomas the Contender**
An uncompromising work which pits Gnosis against the 'bit' of the world
which leads men on down the stream of unconsciousness until 'it has fettered
them'. We are to have wings to fly above the shame and degradation of
worldly death-life.

Codex Three

1. *The Apocryphon of John*
A shorter version of the aforementioned work.
2. *The Gospel of the Egyptians*
A most esoteric work which employs now undecipherable symbolism and
imagery. A sense of incomprehensible ecstasy pervades.
3. *Eugnostos, the Blessed*
A description of the unknown God and the primal 'Son of Man' who is
androgynous. This is not a Christian work and testifies thereby to the
existence of non-Christian Gnosis which is, in the following work, seen to
interpenetrate the thought of Christian Gnostics.
4. *The Sophia of Jesus Christ*
'Sophia' means Wisdom, and the Christian Gnostic feels able to claim Christ
as the origin of non-Christian Gnosis, though this is not explicit in the text.
The disciples pose questions and the Wisdom of Jesus in the flesh answers –
perhaps not to our satisfaction.
5. *The Dialogue of the Saviour*
Fragmentary account of Jesus answering the *big* questions which the disciples
now feel able to ask him following the resurrection. Jesus talks about the
origin of the universe, the nature of the heavenly world and material per-
taining to salvation. The disciples now exclaim their delight at understanding
the *real* meaning behind some of the canonical parables.

Codex Four

1. *The Apocryphon of John*
Another copy. This work must have been very popular among
Gnostics.
2. *The Gospel of the Egyptians*
Again, another copy – with some textual variants.

Codex Five

1. *Eugnostos the Blessed*
Very similar to the aforementioned text.
2. *The Apocalypse of Paul*
Rather fragmentary account of Paul's journey to the 'tenth heaven'. Clearly
inspired by Paul's account of a journey to the third heaven in II Corinthians,

this text takes him and the reader *all* the way. He is led by a small child (the Logos?) through the heavens. At the seventh, he has to talk his way on by answering correctly a question put to him by an old man clothed in white. Paul says, 'I am going to the place from which I came.' On passing to the tenth heaven, 'I greeted my fellow spirits,' says 'Paul'.

3. *The First Apocalypse of James**
Describes a discussion between Jesus and James the Just, both before and after the Crucifixion. James says he has been concerned for Jesus but Jesus says the Crucifixion was in reality, only an appearance and that he is glorified by it, not degraded. 'James' says of Jesus:

> You have come with knowledge,
> that you might rebuke their forgetfulness.
> You have come with recollection,
> that you might rebuke their ignorance.

4. *The Second Apocalypse of James*
A collection of poetic and hymnic words delivered by the redeemer who is Jesus via James to the Gnostic community.

5. *The Apocalypse of Adam*
'Seth' is the bearer of redemptive gnosis in this non-Christian work which describes the paradise of Adam and Eve and the fall into ignorance and illusion. They are rescued by three men who reveal the fate that awaits the children of Seth in the future. This work can be used to illustrate the argument that early Gnosticism develops out of Jewish Apocalyptic gnosis prevalent at the time of Jesus and for two or three hundred years before Him. Apocalyptic revelatory gnosis demands that the author be taken up or that he makes an ascent to the source of the divine will where the future is, as it were, made.

Codex Six

1. *The Acts of Peter and the Twelve Apostles*
An account of a sea voyage by Peter and his fellow disciples relates a meeting with a *pearl* peddler who, it transpires, is Jesus. As a peddler, Jesus was not recognized by the rich men of the city but is 'glorified in the churches'.

2. *The Thunder: Perfect Mind*
In a state of 'perfect mind' which erupts into the cosmos of the author, he writes a series of paradoxical statements made by and about the person of a female figure, presumably a projection of the divine Spirit. Much food for thought here. Strangely akin to Jung's work of self-therapy in a period of dislocation: 'Seven Sermons to the Dead', which was written under the pseudonym of 'Basilides' a Gnostic teacher in second century Alexandria.

3. *Authoritative Teaching*
The plight of the soul in a hostile world is here adumbrated in image and symbol.

4. *The concept of Our Great Power*

A series of catastrophes are described from which the redeemed souls shall be preserved; while 'we have acted according to our birth in the flesh, in the creation of the archons, which gives law'. 'We have also come to be in the unchangeable aeon.'

5. *Plato's Republic*

Extremely fragmentary, appallingly translated extract from Plato's dark masterpiece (588b – 589b).

6. *On the Eighth and Ninth**

A dialogue whereby Hermes Trismegistos guides his 'son' (pupil) in the ascent to heavenly spheres of perception and understanding, and knowledge: 'For thy love has reached us.' 'Right, O my son.'

7. *The Prayer of Thanksgiving**

Hermetic prayer of thanksgiving for illuminations gratefully received. Also known in Greek and Latin versions. Part of the cultic liturgy of Hermetic coteries?

8. *Asklepios**

This extract from the Dialogue of Hermes & Asklepios is very important. Formerly, it was known only in a corrupt Latin version (translation attributed to Apuleius of Madaura). This extract contains the extraordinary lament for a barbarized world where formerly men delighted in the 'many formed vision of God'. This was to deeply touch a fifteenth-century Florence where men attempted to rebuild the antiquity referred to, as they saw it. Furthermore, the appearance of the Hermetic works in the Nag Hammadi Library reinforces the conviction that Hermetism is gnostic and cannot be excluded from that study.

Codex Seven

1. *The Paraphrase of Shem*

According to Frederick Wisse, this work can greatly contribute to an understanding of New Testament Christology (the nature of Christ's person and work). It is non-Christian and possibly pre-Christian in origins and describes saving gnosis being given to the children of Shem by one Derdekeas who descends from the Light having taken pity on the entrapped light within the spiritual descendants of Shem. Shem is the narrator and describes the conflict between Light and Darkness and Spirit. Derdekeas experiences the hostility of the world of Darkness but goes unrecognised because he puts on the 'beast', doubtless the body. The elect are saved.

2. *The Second Treatise of the Great Seth**

A Christian Gnostic text which amongst other things has Jesus explaining that it was not He who was put to death on the cross, but another. It only *seemed* that he suffered to the hylic (material) eye. Spiritual vision would have beheld the true nature of the event – a victory over the archons. Jesus was 'rejoicing over all the wealth of the archons'. Within the work is a description of true Gnostic fellowship which begs repetition here:

'I was among those who are united in the friendship of friends forever, who neither know hostility at all, nor evil, but who are united by my Knowledge in word and peace which exists in perfection with everyone and in them all. And those who assumed the form of my type will assume the form of my word. Indeed, these will come forth in light forever, and (in) friendship with each other in the spirit, since they have known in every respect (and) indivisibly that what is is One.

3. *The Apocalypse of Peter**
Here we find the 'laughing Saviour' explaining to Peter what really happened at the crucifixion. The work suggests the existence of a Gnostic church having difficulty in surviving, opposed by orthodox bishops. The writer envisions Jesus who says, encouragingly: 'And there shall be others of those who are outside our number who name themselves bishop and also deacons, as if they have received their authority from God. They bend themselves under the judgement of the leaders. Those people are dry canals.' *Dry* canals. One can imagine what this term would mean to a thirsty man dwelling in a parched Egypt. I suppose today's equivalent expression would be *empty banks*.

4. *The Teachings of Silvanus*
A philosophical work, acceptable to Gnostics but not for them in particular, it gives recommendations on how to subdue the senses of the body and to find guidance from a teacher of light, Christ. God is difficult to know except through his 'image' and one is reminded of the Hermetic master-phrase: 'The world is the image of God.'

5. *The Three Steles of Seth*
Non-Christian Sethian Gnostic work contains hymns presumably employed by the sect as aids to meditation.

Codex Eight

1. *Zostrianos*
A work of this name was known to Porphyry in the third century. This text is extremely fragmentary but if one 'reads between the spaces' one can detect a revelatory journey to Zostrianos by an angel of knowledge and others.

2. *The Letter of Peter to Philip*
Pseudonymous 'letter' introduction soon reveals itself as typical Gnostic revelation discourse.

Codex Nine

1. *Melchizedek*
Gnostics and apocalyptic writers always loved the shadowy and mysterious persons who appear in ancient religious writing. Melchizedek, king of Salem (Peace), played host to Abraham. According to Psalm cx.4 he was a 'priest forever', and such an eternal type was sure to give rise to speculation, some of which is to be found in the canonical Epistle to the Hebrews where Christ

is seen as the absolute high-priest who has effected the ultimate sacrifice. In this Gnostic work, Melchizedek is privy to heavenly messages which culminate in him seeing himself in the role of Jesus Christ as triumphant victor over 'Death'. The author seems to identify the Gnostic with Melchizedek: 'When the brethren who belong to the generations of life had said these things, they were taken up to (the regions) above all the heavens.'

2. *The Thought of Norea*
A short poetic work describing a female entity, Norea, within the Pleroma, among Logos and Nous.

3. *The Testimony of Truth*
The 'true testimony' that is as against other groups both Gnostic and orthodox. Only for those who 'hear not with the ears of the body but with the ears of the mind.'

Codex Ten

1. *Marsanes*
Very badly damaged. This work was also known to Porphyry, follower of Plotinus, or at least a work of this name. It contains or did contain a grand description of the heavenly world – the kind of thing a magician in particular might wish to know. Birger A. Pearson sees it as having affinities to Neoplatonism and thinks it might represent a shift away from a rigidly dualist position to the projecting monism of Neoplatonism.

Codex Eleven

1. *The Interpretation of Knowledge*
A sermon with a Valentinian colouring. According to Elaine Pagels: 'Strikingly, this teacher develops an interpretation of knowledge rather similar to that of Paul in I Corinthians XIII or even of I John. Unlike Paul or the author of I John, however, this teacher offers a specifically Gnostic interpretation, implying that those who show jealousy and hatred betray their resemblance to the jealous and ignorant demiurge, while those who show love demonstrate the love of God the Father and of his Word.'

2. *A Valentinian Exposition*
This work contains detailed exposition of Valentinian thought regarding the eucharist, anointing and baptism and gives us an insiders-look into Valentinian church prayer practice. The sacraments are vehicles for coming to understand the mystery of Christ and Life itself.

3. *Allogenes*
The title means 'alien' or 'stranger' and thereby expresses the fundamental attitude of the Gnostic to the material world as material. Allogenes gives his pupil Messos an esoteric disclosure of the Unknown.

4. *Hypsiphrone*
This is too fragmentary to say anything about it other than that it is a revelation discourse given by 'She of High Mind'.

Codex Twelve

1. *The Sentences of Sextus*
   This a Greek work here translated into Coptic which offers wisdom sayings chiefly aimed at mastering the passions. Much would be music to the ear of the Gnostic: 'Do not wish to speak in a crowd about God ... Know who God is, and know who is the one who thinks in you; a good man is the good work of God.'
2. *The Gospel of Truth*
   A short fragment of the aforementioned work.
3. *Unidentified fragments*

Codex Thirteen

1. *Trimorphic Protennoia*
   The *Protennoia*, the 'First Thought' of the Father speaks in the first-person to describe his/her (*Protennoia* being androgynous), descents into the world where he/she speaks to the 'sons of the Thought'. *Protennoia* describes him/herself as 'the Unchanging Sound'. In my opinion, there is something distasteful if not sinister in this work.
2. *On the Origin of the World*
   A short section from the beginning of the aforementioned treatise of this name.

Appendix Three

Joseph Ritman, the Star and the Library of the Light

Some readers may wonder what all this gnosis business has to do with the modern world – what real *use* is it? In a sense, I should like readers to ask that question of themselves. Nevertheless, I thought it might be both instructive and interesting to reproduce an interview I conducted with a man who has applied gnosis to business with staggering success. If one thinks that the source of his success can be traced to no more than a strong and intuitive business sense, that is entirely reasonable. On the other hand, Joseph Ritman's attitude to business is deeply suffused by gnosis – and who knows where one begins and the other ends?

Joseph Ritman sees himself as a benefactor to mankind. In his vision, service is the only mode of action which will bear fruit in our times. Mr Ritman's service has been to open up his extraordinary library to an enquiring public. In 1984, the Hermetic Philosophy Library was fully institutionalized. With the profits made by his company *De Ster* (The Star), he has been a serious collector of esoteric works in book and manuscript form. Many of these works are first editions and are extremely rare. Mr Ritman's dream is to assemble the most complete collection of Rosicrucian, Hermetic, Alchemical, Mystical, Neo-platonist and ancient Gnostic Sources that can be achieved. Joseph Ritman spends his time, when not travelling on business, moving between the *Ster* offices and the library, his first love, and for which the 'Star' exists primarily to support. The 'Star,' incidentally, is the world's largest producer of plastic disposables for airlines in the world. Next time you catch a plane from London, Birmingham, Paris, Amsterdam, Frankfurt, New York or Hong Kong, take a look at the dishes and cutlery in which your meal is served. If you find a little five-pointed star embossed on the items, know that you have made an indirect contribution to the *Bibliotheca Philosophica Hermetica*!

The principle on which Mr Ritman operates is that of the gnostic intuition of a universal 'cross' of communication. The horizontal line respresents the material, temporal plane on which we spend our lives. Ritman's gnosis consists, in principle, of seizing the point of intersection where a spiritual 'ray' of energy touches the material plane. Life is then a confident struggle to balance the material and the spiritual, while keeping the fire of the inner 'sun' burning in the darkness of matter, illuminating the path to God. Ritman sees his business as essentially one of *communication* and he gains great inspiration from the image of Hermes. Hermes moves where he wills, he is the messenger of the gods moving in 'air' with wings on feet and head – so expressing the liberty of the Hermetic *mens* or mind. The Hermetic magus weds the material earth to the spiritual heaven, as Pico della Mirandola maintained. He must penetrate the *image* of the world to the reality beyond. In simple terms, life for a modern gnostic, Mr Ritman maintains, consists in the transformation of life by the putting to service of material things, no matter how small, to spiritual ends – from tiny acorns mighty oaks do grow! Joseph Ritman's first acorn was a copy of *Aurora* by the shoemaker of Gorlitz, Jacob Boehme – given to him by his mother when he was a young man. 'Young man' – what am I saying? – Joseph Ritman millionaire-gnostic, is only forty-six today! 'Man is a great miracle, O Asclepius, is his watchword.

We met among the sturdy oak panels of that part of the *Ster* offices built in the manner of the Dutch seventeenth century on 5 June 1986. Scenes from the Bible are carved into the ornate cupboards and panels. Below us is a fountain about a statue of Hermes. His finger points upwards to the words inscribed in gold on marble, which, when translated, read: 'God is an infinite sphere whose centre is everywhere and circumference nowhere.' I began by asking of the *meaning* of the 'Ster' offices:

J.R.: I think that with these offices I go back to the 'rijk' (rich) tradition of Holland. Holland in the seventeenth century was a very powerful country, very active in the sea-trade and these offices are a point of reference to that. I would like to bridge that very rich period with the sea trade to the period we're living in now, so we say OK, our customers are in a modern situation, they represent a new point, a new bridge of communication – no longer the sea but the *air*. And what we like is to identify ourselves as traditional Dutch merchants and we like to give our visitors who come from all over the world an idea of how rich we were and how we see our modern responsibility. We receive you with your problems for communication in the air but we like to receive that in the quiet atmosphere of the Dutch seventeenth century – and with these offices we give them the feeling of that powerful time.

The other side, we have not only seventeenth century rooms but also modern offices, so it's a combination between tradition and being very modern, very rational, very accurate. Traditional impulse in a new period – that's what it means. The philosophy of our company also has its roots in the philosophy of Holland that has three aspects in the seventeenth century which were very meaningful: love, hope and faith. With these three aspects, one finds them also in the art of the seventeenth century and the inner meaning of the seventeenth century. We believe that now it is still powerful to work with love, hope and faith.

AUTHOR: What does the *Ster* factory mean to you?

J.R.: I'm very proud of the factory. It's a leading producer in the world, producing 50 million articles with the Star on them. I was always interested in communicating with the world. I was always interested in travel – to meet people. I believe that we're solving the problems of our clients from all corners of the world. We created an enormous possibility in having that factory and if you say 'what is the meaning of it?' – it means service to our clients – and with our factory, we developed a total organism to solve all the problems in the air nowadays – and we serve with our plastics; they are used by passengers all over the world. I can say that by having the factory, in the western world, we're serving 60 per cent of the airline industry – you can't board a plane in England without seeing our products. I believe that with my factory, I've proved my conviction to communicate with leading airline institutes of the world – my personal interest in communication. Starting in Holland with the catering industry, going from the early ships to the airline industry of nowadays, we are very proud of the philosophy of service in a period where airline communication came to life around fifteen or twenty years ago – it is now a common habit for people to travel this way. We have the tools in this factory to make our conviction to do something for the world – and to gain the possibilities to transform them again in the world of my library.

AUTHOR: It might be difficult to understand how spiritual life can go hand in hand with the ultra-technological facilities that you employ and the use to which they're put. Can you explain a bit how international communications can relate to the inner world?

J.R.: I believe the confirmation is in the practice. At a given moment, you can develop the technical developments in a way that you have your men linked to a material aspect. A material aspect which goes together with technique, with products, with customers, with the world itself. At a certain moment if you follow that logic, the globe is not so immense any more. The same moment you find that within yourself is a spiritual world that in a way is free of time, free of limitations, free in itself. It gives you a continuous impulse to see the reality in which a spiritual and a material life go together. And the secret is in being itself, being a man who proves to the world that you can build a library and that you can build a factory with a worldwide effect.

AUTHOR: Do you think more people in the modern world are learning that secret?

J.R.: Yes. I think that the technical world has come to a border that is impossible to pass without the acceptance that the impulse, the drive of life in itself, always comes from an invisible spiritual level. I believe that in the technical world they discovered secrets of the atom in a technical way. They can develop shuttles to the moon, but there is no answer to the very beginning of the impulse itself. In the ancient world, it was understood that man has to climb or to go into himself in an inner development to find the secret key which answers *the* question with: I know where I come from, I know why I am here, and I know my destiny.

AUTHOR: We've made a link: sitting on an aeroplane having a meal and reading a book. The Hermetic library, where does it fit in? From eating to gnosis!

J.R.: I believe that people travel for a reason – that they have something to do with someone else. In the past it was very difficult to travel, so man was connected to a place, a small community. We are now living in a time where these problems are solved through the development of the airline industry, so it's not so strange that there is a relationship between an airplane and a library. As a matter of fact, I never travel without a book of my library and I know that the works of real value were always transported on a camel or a ship; perhaps we are now in a period when we transport them via aeroplanes.

The most striking point is that the human being of nowadays finds very strongly – he knows that in the last 2,000 years time was divided in periods or in impulses in cities or countries but now he knows that all these spiritual traditions come together, and if you make the bridge to my library – there is not only the river of Life – there is a *Sea* of Life: that wisdom which was floated already over the globe; with the horse; with the seaship, and now an airship – is also the proof that the spirit of my library, the Hermetic spirit, the Gnostic spirit, is *free* in a way of limitations, transportations. Why free? Because the human being, in a place or country or sitting in my library, can experience that spiritual climate that you can find in a book, find in a library. We now come to the conviction that it is not only in a book or library or in person. I think that this spirit, you can say, is *in the air*, it's everywhere – and if you link my library and factory, I say that my factory is a modern aspect of what you *believe*, what you can *do*, what this energy, this insight, this conviction and also this optimism in life can give you in your hands to connect your self to the past, the value of the present, where you live; that with the contents of that wisdom, not something that is behind us but which is *with* us, with this power, this energy, you can change the world. My library is an instrument, but what it proves is the value of life. In one aspect: the tradition – what brought us so far, why we are comfortable in this part of the world, but in another, it shows us the next step which we have to take to enter into a new period where we have to change the world together! This tradition has proved its value. If we try to speak about the gnosis or the Hermetic philosophy, we see that it is not a dead subject but is a very active and vivid subject that we can discuss together.

I also think that with Gnosticism, what you are planning to do in your film to show where that river streamed through time, now, in a modern world you can say OK, it's a changing power, it will give the world a new dimension – I call it the fifth dimension, the 'ether' of Plato – that there is a world-field of activity, of energy and also of spiritual tradition. I believe that this vertical power-field which comes to the earth will also give a new effect to the horizontal expression of the power.

I believe that in the second and third centuries, the time of the early Gnostics, they did not see the world as a fact in itself but they saw this invisible world, all these aspects of the hierarchy of spirituality. It was not something that was beyond time, or beyond their life, no, it was very active *in* their life. I believe that nowadays, the real leaders of the world, they live with the absolute conviction that there is something more than life as we know it right now. As the result of our tradition, this comes to a physical thing. If you say then, how do I see my library? In the same way as my factory – *communication*.

AUTHOR: Would you see it as a higher level than the factory?

J.R.: My library? I see it as an *inner* level, going inward to human beings, bringing people together. Two weeks ago I met the Dalai Lama who was here in Holland. I was invited to speak with him and it is not only the Dalai Lama, we are also communicating with the Vatican Library and the British Library and the Bibliothèque Nationale. We are having exhibitions – we had one in Ravenna, Italy, in the early spring. In summer, we are in Venice with our books – and that is a whole world of communication!

AUTHOR: How do you feel about the Cathars and Montségur?

J.R.: It was the real impulse in my life. When I was sixteen years old, I went for the first time to the South of France. I visited Montségur and there I very strongly felt that there was a brotherhood who were very active with the philosophy of the early Gnostics. I found for myself the confirmation of a power-field, a very active power-field of enormous spiritual value to Western Europe.

Montségur was built on a place where in former times there was a solar temple – the architecture also of these castles in the south of France, they were connected to the solar solstice points in June and December. In a way, the wisdom of the Cathars was in one aspect *purification* of the Catholic Church, but also going back to the early period of the Greek mysteries and Egyptian mysteries, the dualistic philosophy of Mani, the early gnosis. All these theories were very active in that time.

I found with the story of the troubadours and the castle of the troubadours and the story of the Knights of the Round Table – and all those stories that were discussed there in the castles in the culture of the period. For myself, in the south of France, I found the earliest roots of the Gnostic tradition in Europe from the year 1000 on. I can therefore say that the south of France brought a peak experience in my life. I saw something that I knew from an inner feeling hidden in myself.

AUTHOR: What is suffering for?

J.R.: Suffering is purification and purification means going back to the real meaning of life. Therefore, I believe that if you suffer, that is a period where you bring one thing to the next thing, you say, OK, you have to climb a mountain but the only reason you suffer is that you will reach the top. And if you say 'what is suffering for?' – it is the price for *value*. The price for an end – goal. The price for asolute freedom. It is *fire*, suffering. So people go through the fire – you believe in the absolute essence, the source of fire, you go for it. I can give you a very nice example. You have that story of Icarus and they say Icarus, he tried to fly to the sun and it's a shame that he fell to earth and was drowned. But I think he was the first man who took the experience very seriously. If you come back to the present – in the early days it was absolutely impossible for a human being to fly to the Sun. We had to live on the earth. The second period showed us making journeys all over the world; man used the sea, and now we are in the third experience of Icarus – we are making use of the air – and then there is a fourth period, what I call the *solar century*, the next century, we will go to the sun! Every human being is capable of going to the real source of energy.

So if you say 'suffering', well if you count together all the sufferings of all human beings so far, it is only purification of the mind, purification of the human experience. *Why?*

AUTHOR: What of the suffering inflicted by others? It's true to say creation is the product of pain – purifies, re-creates, transforms, but surely there is no value in suffering unjustly inflicted?

J.R.: I don't believe in injustice. In the moment that there is an injustice, a conflict in your life – I believe it comes to you as a *shock* – but only to guide you – that you have to believe in yourself, you have to find the balance in your life. There is no end-goal in the human personality, there is no end-goal in the human body, there is no end-goal in visible things, in time and space and even in the universe – there is only an end-goal in the invisible spirituality that we feel, that is the driving power in our life. There has to be an absolute integration between spirit and matter – and I believe that the end of suffering is at the opening of the chrysalis, the butterfly. I think the process has a certain value. At a certain moment you are free from your body, that matter is free from itself, and it can move to the Sun.

So to conclude all the elements of this discussion, to take the offices as a proof, to take the factory as a proof, to take the library as a proof, I can only say that it is a living matter, a living energy that is everywhere in my life so that in all the aspects of your personal life, of your spiritual life, of your life in the community, you bring that value to each moment, to each occasion, then you bring the secret of the gnosis. That's it!

Bibliography

Agrippa, Henry Cornelius, *De Occulta Philosophia* (London, 1651).

Aligarh Journal of English Studies. Vol. 1. 1976. No. 2. 'Blake and the Gnostic Legends' by Piloo Nanavutty.

The Ante-Nicene Fathers. Translated by Roberts and Donaldson (Eerdmans Publishing Company, Michigan, 1981).

The Asclepius. Translated and edited by Nock and Festugière.

Barbarini, Cullman, and Graustark. *Strawberry Fields Forever: John Lennon Remembered* (Bantam, 1980).

Biblical Archaeologist (Fall, 1979).

Bohm, David, *Wholeness and the Implicate Order* (Routledge and Kegan Paul, 1981).

Burkitt, F. C., *Church and Gnosis* (University Cambridge Press, 1932).

Casaubon, Meric, *A strange relation of what passed between Dr John Dee and some spirits* (1659).

Chadwick, Henry, *The Early Church* (Pelican, 1978).

The Confessions of Aleister Crowley. Edited by Symonds and Grant (Routledge and Kegan Paul, 1979).

Dee, John, *Monas Hieroglyphica* (Antwerp, 1564).

Documents of the Christian Church. Edited by Henry Bettenson (Oxford, 1977).

Doresse, Jean, *The Secret Books of the Egyptian Gnostics* (Hollis & Carter, 1960).

Eusebius Ecclesiastical History. Translated by Kirsopp Lake (Loeb Classical Library, 1975).

French, Peter, *John Dee* (Routledge and Kegan Paul, 1972).

Gnosticism: An Anthology. Edited by R. M. Grant (Collins, 1961).

Henderson, David, *Scuse me while I kiss the sky* (Bantam, 1981).

The Heptarchia Mystica of John Dee. Edited by Robert Turner (Aquarian Press, 1986).

Hermetica. Translated by Walter Scott (Shambhala Press, 1986).

The Hermetick Art. By a lover of Philalethes (London, 1714).

Holy Bible. Revised version. Oxford.

Inge, William Ralph, *The Philosophy of Plotinus* (Longmans).

Jonas, Hans, *The Imperative of Responsibility* (University of Chicago, 1984); and *Philosophical Essays From Ancient Creed to Technological Man* (University of Chicago, 1980). *The Gnostic Religion* (Beacon Press, 1958).

Journal de Centre Nationale d'études Cathares. 'Heresis. 1–5' (1984–6).

Journal of Historical Studies. 'The Albigensian Crusade' by Bernard Hamilton.

Jung, C. G., *Psychology and Alchemy* (Routledge and Kegan Paul, 1981).

Kelley, J. N. D., *Early Christian Doctrines* (A. and C. Black, 1977).

Klibansky, Saxl and Panofsky, *Saturn and Melancholy* (Nelson).

Klonsky, Milton, *Blake's Dante* (Sidgwick and Jackson, 1980).

Knight, Gareth, *A History of White Magic* (Mowbrays, 1978).

Lefebure, Molly, *Samuel Taylor Coleridge: A Bondage of Opium* (Quartet, 1977).

Lennon, John, *Skywriting by Word of Mouth* (Pan Books in association with Jonathan Cape, 1986).

Le Livre des Deux Principes. Edited by Christine Thouzellier. (Editions du Cerf, 1973.)

Mahé, Jean Pierre, *Hermès en Haute Egypte.* 2 vols. (University of Quebec Press, 1978; 1982).

The Metamorphosis or Golden Ass and Philosophical works of Apuleius. Translated by Thomas Taylor.

Moore, R. I., *Origins of European Dissent* (Basil Blackwell, 1985).

Morley, Henry, *The Life of H. C. Agrippa.* 2 vols. (Chapman and Hall, 1856).

Morrison, Jim, *The Lords and the New Creatures* (Simon and Schuster, 1971).

Motta, Marcelo, *The Commentaries of AL. Aleister Crowley* (Routledge and Kegan Paul, 1976).

The Nag Hammadi Library. Edited by James M. Robinson (E. J. Brill, Leiden, 1977).

New Testament and Gnosis. Edited by A. H. B. Logan and A. J. M. Wedderburn (T. & T. Clark Limited, 1983).

Newton, Sir Isaac, *Observations upon the Prophecies of Daniel and the Apocalypse of John. In Two Parts* (1733).

Occult and Scientific Mentalities in the Renaissance. Edited by Brian Vickers (University Cambridge Press, 1984).

Of the vanitie and uncertaintie of Artes and Sciences. English ed by Ja. San. Gent. Henry Wykes Fleete Streat. Anno. 1569.

Oldenburg, Zoe, *The Massacre of Montségur.*

Pagels, Elaine, *The Gnostic Gospels* (Weidenfeld and Nicolson, 1980).

The Philosophy of Plato. Book One. Apuleius of Madaura. Translated by Thomas Taylor.

The Poems of William Blake. Edited by W. B. Yeats (Routledge and Kegan Paul, 1979).

Quispel, Gilles, *Gnostic Studies,* 2 vols (Leiden, 1974, 1975).

Raine, Kathleen, *Blake and Antiquity* (Routledge and Kegan Paul, 1979).

The Renaissance Philisophy of Man. Edited by Kristeller and E. Cassirer (University of Chicago, 1948).

Rocquebert, Michel, *Cathar Castles* (1985); and *En Face de Catharisme* (Cahiers de Fanjeaux, 1984).

Rudolph, Kurt, *Gnosis* (Harper and Row, 1985).

Runciman, Steven, *The Medieval Manichee* (Cambridge University Press, 1984).

Scholem, Gershom, *Major Trends in Jewish Mysticism* (Schocken Books, 1961).

Select Works of Plotinus. Translated by Thomas Taylor. Edited by G. R. S. Mead (Bohm's Popular Library, 1914).

Shakespeare, William, *The Tempest* (Penguin, 1985).

Shelley, Mary, *Frankenstein* (Oxford, 1980).

Singer, Dorothea, *Giordano Bruno – His Life and Thought with annotated translations of his work On the Infinite Universe and Worlds* (Schuman, 1950).

Weiser, Samuel, *The Hieroglyphic Monad. Dr John Dee*. Translated by J. Hamilton-Jones (1977).

Wilson, Mona, *The Life of William Blake* (Paladin/Granada, 1978).

Wilson, R. McL., *The Gnostic Problem* (Mowbray, 1958); *Gnosis and the New Testament* (Blackwell, 1968).

Yamauchi, Edwin, *Pre-Christian Gnosticism* (Tyndale Press, 1973).

Yates, Frances, *Astraea*; *Giordano Bruno and the Hermetic Tradition*; *The Occult Philosophy in the Elizabethan Age*; *The Rosicrucian Enlightenment*; *Shakespeare's Last Plays* (all Routledge and Kegan Paul).

Zachner, R. C., *Our Savage God* (Collins, 1974).

Index